JACK SHELTON'S
HOW TO ENJOY 1 TO 10
PERFECT DAYS IN
SAN FRANCISCO

JACK SHELTON'S HOW TO ENJOY 1 TO 10 PERFECT DAYS IN SAN FRANCISCO

Completely updated and expanded by
JACK R. JUHASZ

FIFTH EDITION

Edited by Dale Richards

SHELTON PUBLICATIONS
BOX 391
SAUSALITO, CALIF. 94966

Library of Congress Catalog Card Number: 90-091697
ISBN 0-918742-04-8

PRINTED IN THE UNITED STATES OF AMERICA

SHELTON PUBLICATIONS
Box 391
Sausalito, California 94966
(415) 332-1165

Contents

5

Introduction

When Jack Shelton and I planned the first edition of this book many years ago, we both wanted to make it as interesting and as unique as the city which is its subject—San Francisco.

Shelton, a transplanted New Yorker, loved San Francisco passionately because to him it represented a less hectic life-style in more beautiful and congenial surroundings. I, as a native San Franciscan, loved it as all natives love and cherish it.

Together, we set out to create a guide book that would put onto paper exactly what we would recommend to you if you were a close friend visiting here for the very first time. To give you the very best this marvelous city has to offer, no matter how short your stay.

Therefore, the first day, for example, presents what we would recommend you do if you had only one day to spend here. If you had two days, we would go on to suggest the second day's activities and so forth.

Because the scheduling involves many arbitrary decisions on our part, times and days are set purely as a guide and should not inhibit you. Switch things around to suit yourself.

We begin with a day-to-day schedule covering one complete, perfect week basically in The City itself. Then for the remaining days, we offer two-, three- or four-day suggested trips to areas easily reached from San Francisco: the Mendocino Coast, Carmel-Monterey and Hearst Castle, and the Napa Valley.

Since dining out in San Francisco is the favorite pastime for native and visitor alike, great emphasis has been placed on restaurant-going. Even though San Francisco is world famous as a "restaurant town," like all such cities it nevertheless possesses a substantial number of terrible "tourist traps." To make sure you not only avoid these but discover the truly fine restaurants (many of which do not advertise aggressively), each day's schedule gives you a variety of selections for both lunch and dinner.

In addition, specific recommendations on what to order insure your getting the best each kitchen has to offer. In choosing these restaurants for you, we have drawn on our twenty-five years of experience as Bay Area restaurant critics. And unlike many other guides, we employ no stringers. *I personally have tested every single one of the dishes at every one of the restaurants described in this book. Without exception.*

What you won't find are those restaurants which appear on all kinds of lists simply because their fame—and not their cuisine—warrants their inclusion. What you will find are over fifty of our personal favorites—some famous, others obscure little "finds"—which will provide you with what we personally consider the finest and most interesting dining experiences in town.

And when that "town" is San Francisco, it means some of the finest and most exciting dining anywhere! As with all other recommended activities, though, let your personal taste and budget be your guide. If you want to switch restaurant visits around or follow a special craving or whim, do so. And to help you do just that, we have included a separate Index of Recommended Restaurants, which lists all the restaurants reviewed in this book by both location and type of cuisine.

Remember: should you find yourself heading home with a lot left to see and experience, do not feel bad. . . there is no such thing as visiting San Francisco only once.

Jack R. Juhasz

PART ONE

One Perfect Week
in San Francisco

Your First Perfect Day Schedule

8:30 a.m. Board a Hyde Street cable car at Powell and Market Streets in front of Woolworth's.

9:00 a.m. Arrive at the last stop and have breakfast at the Buena Vista Cafe, corner of Beach and Hyde Streets.

10:00 a.m. After breakfast, stroll to Ghirardelli Square, Aquatic Park, the Maritime Museum, Hyde Street Pier, The Cannery and Fisherman's Wharf.

11:45 a.m. Hop a Powell Street cable car and either get off at Pacific Avenue for a "dim sum" lunch at a tiny Chinatown hideaway followed by a walk through Chinatown; remain on board until Union Square and lunch at trendy Postrio; or—if it has reopened—lunch in the breathtaking Garden Court of the historic Palace Hotel.

2:00 p.m. Pick up your rental car for the 49-Mile Drive, or take Gray Line's City Tour #1.

7:00 p.m. Cocktails at the Top of the Mark.

8:00 p.m. A short stroll around Nob Hill.

8:30 p.m. Luxurious French, exciting Mediterranean *cum* California, or vivacious Vietnamese are your culinary options for dinner tonight.

11:00 p.m. A classy cabaret act, a deafening disco, or the latest stand-up comic's shtick.

2:00 a.m. If you are still up, a goodnight view of San Francisco from the top of Telegraph Hill; or, if you are hungry again, a visit to the "Coca Cola" restaurant.

How to Spend One Perfect Day
in San Francisco

8:30 a.m. Welcome to your first day in San Francisco! I hope the sun is brightly shining. If it's foggy, don't let that worry you too much. Fog is a natural condition of San Francisco mornings, especially in the summer months. And more than likely it will burn off by noon.

Don't even look at that room service menu, because we are off to breakfast at a San Francisco institution. All you have to do is find Market Street. That shouldn't be too hard, since it is the main thoroughfare of downtown San Francisco.

You actually want the corner of Powell and Market. Because right there in front of a massive Woolworth's store you will find what millions upon millions of children and adults have traveled halfway around the world to see—the famous San Francisco cable cars.

At this early hour, the wait should not be long. So get a ticket and hop aboard a "Powell and Hyde Street" car—it's the one with the maroon sign on the roof. If you are not sure you have the right car, ask for the one that goes to Aquatic Park *not* Fisherman's Wharf. Weather permitting, try to get an outside seat on the right-hand (Woolworth's) side.

By sitting on the outside section, you will be privileged to watch the gripman as he runs the car. You will quickly discover that cable car gripmen and fare collectors are a breed unto themselves with extraordinarily open personalities. During your over-the-hills ride, you may see them interrupt a flirtation with a pretty young passenger to chastise an impatient motorist with such remarks as, "You dare honk your horn at a national historical monument?" For indeed that is what these rickety wooden trolleys are.

You also cannot help noticing their special pride and warmth about being the ones who give life to that historical monument, and they will readily answer any questions you may have about the cable car.

However, in case you are shy, let me explain that the cable car runs with the aid of a continuously moving cable (9 1/2-miles-per-hour) located below the street. The street contains an open slot the entire length of the run, and the car has clamps which extend into the slot and fasten onto the cable below to propel the car forward. Releasing the grip stops the car. It cannot back up, but it does have a braking mechanism. In addition, the cable car triggers a device which causes traffic lights on hills to turn green as it approaches. Cross traffic stops so the car can make it to the top. Cable cars contain no electricity and the lights are operated by a battery.

Now, here we go up Powell Street, eight stops to the top of Nob Hill. From a right-hand seat, you will get an exciting look down California Street past Chinatown to the Bay. Twisting your neck to look out the other side of the car will show you the famed Fairmont and Mark Hopkins Hotels, both of which you will see more closely later in the day.

Another few blocks and the gripman warns you to hang on as the car first swings left and then soon rounds another curve onto Hyde Street heading toward Russian Hill. Here, the car again starts climbing and in a few moments, you will see two of the most thrilling views in all the world.

The first will present itself to you at the top of Lombard Street, "the crookedest street in the world." (Notice how the street curves several times around flower beds.) Your view will be eastward toward Telegraph Hill, capped with Coit Tower, and the Bay with the Bay Bridge connecting San Francisco to the East Bay.

Soon, a turn of your head forward and slightly to the left will give you a panoramic view of the Golden Gate Bridge. Then a deep breath as the car goes down the hill—a glance at Alcatraz Island right in front of you and a feeling of relief when the car stops at its final destination, Beach Street.

Here you will get off and find yourself in front of the

Buena Vista Cafe, 2765 Hyde (474-5044; open weekdays from 9 a.m.; weekends from 8 a.m.). And even if the doors have just opened, do not be surprised if you find a line already formed.

9:00 a.m.   Enter the Buena Vista Cafe, find a table overlooking the charming Victorian Park with its cable car turntable and the waterfront beyond, and immediately order (service can be slow when crowded) a fine, hearty breakfast with one of the Buena Vista world-famous Irish Coffees as a finale. Of course, if you have a few encores of this concoction, which was introduced to the United States in 1953 right on this spot, your first perfect day in San Francisco may start and finish at the Buena Vista. However, I can think of far worse fates!

To begin your breakfast, ask for another B.V. favorite, their velvety New Orleans Fizz. The rest of breakfast is traditional—eggs with excellent sausage or ham or bacon, served with hashed-and-browned potatoes. Everything is cooked to order, which accounts for much of the often-encountered waits, and the eggs are especially well prepared. The leisurely, mellow Irish Coffee conclusion will make this a breakfast you will long remember, if the mood captures you.

I know it might be difficult to think of lunch and dinner right at this moment but in San Francisco, where reservations are required in almost all important restaurants, you have to do just that.

As a matter of fact, because top restaurants often are booked solid far in advance, it really would be best if you read the reviews of the restaurants in this guide as soon as you can. Then sit down and call all the restaurants you wish to visit. San Franciscans take dining out seriously and think nothing of reserving weeks in advance.

For lunch today, I have three recommendations—a tiny inexpensive Chinatown spot, where you can savor delightful dim sum (Chinese luncheon tidbits) in an informal atmosphere; or Postrio, a chic showplace near Union Square with a crowd as trendy as its eclectic *nouvelle* California cuisine menu; or one of the world's most beautiful dining rooms, the Garden Court of the Palace Hotel.

As far as the food in the Garden Court is concerned, I cannot comment on it. For as I write these words, the Palace Hotel is undergoing a complete renovation and will not reopen for months. Because the Garden Court is a registered landmark, I cannot see how it can be changed. And since the food served there prior to the renovation was "hotel food" at its most faceless, I cannot see how it could worsen.

So read ahead for my full descriptions of these unique lunch spots before making up your mind. No reservations are accepted at the dim sum house, but if you opt for Postrio or the Garden Court, you should call for a 12:30 p.m. reservation before you leave the Buena Vista.

For dinner, I offer three suggestions, giving you three vastly different cuisines in three different price ranges. The first is Fleur de Lys (673-7779; reservations imperative), my favorite top-drawer French restaurant where sensational cuisine is suavely presented in a very elegant—and expensive—ambience.

My second: Square One (788-1110; reservations a must) is an exciting restaurant where the culinary repertory of primarily the Mediterranean is enhanced by inventive California touches and served at upper moderate prices.

And my third suggestion is Golden Turtle (441-4419; reservations recommended) where tantalizing Vietnamese cuisine is presented in an upscale setting at modest prices.

If none of these three personal favorites appeals to you for this evening, you will find a complete listing of all my recommended restaurants in the back.

And there are some other arrangements you must also make now. For this afternoon's activity, I recommend seeing the city either by car—by driving San Francisco's popular 49-Mile Drive—or by tour bus.

Therefore, if you are planning to do the driving yourself, you might wish to telephone your favorite rental car company to make certain they will have a car for you this afternoon at about 2:00 p.m. Once all these necessary phone calls are completed, you can start your walking tour of the Fisherman's Wharf area.

10:00 a.m.   When you leave the Buena Vista Cafe, turn left and walk one block down Beach Street. Here you will find Ghirardelli Square, a colorful shopping-dining complex created from an old chocolate factory.

Most American cities, especially tourist-conscious ones, have some kind of historic edifice which has been converted into a shopping-dining complex. San Francisco has two exceptional examples within a few blocks of one another—The Cannery and Ghirardelli Square.

The latter, which happens to be my favorite, was designed as a factory complex in 1893; and for 70 years, this 2 1/2-acre site was the home of the Ghirardelli Chocolate Company. When the chocolate makers moved, the massive brick complex could have been leveled to make way for another high rise for the well-heeled.

But thanks to civic-minded William Matson Roth, the ancient buildings marked by the quaint clock tower, curiously a copy of the Chateau Blois in France, were converted into a warren of shops and eateries, opening onto a sunny piazza with a whimsical Ruth Asawa fountain. As I understand it, the original shops and restaurants came to the square by invitation only. Shops range from the trendy Sharper Image to folk-art galleries. For kids of all ages there are exotic kites and cuddly stuffed animals. A remarkable melange. And the Square is also the home of The Mandarin, generally regarded as the city's top pan-Chinese restaurant, which we will visit tomorrow night.

Across the street is Aquatic Park and the Maritime Museum (open daily 10:00 a.m. to 5 p.m.). If you have youngsters along, they'll be thrilled with the huge sea anchors and other ocean-going memorabilia on display at the museum; and be sure to show them the intricate miniature clipper ships and freighters.

After leaving the museum, walk down onto the beach for a partial view of the Golden Gate Bridge—provided the fog is not in! On the beach, turn right, back toward the

Victorian Park and down Jefferson Street. Just past the South End Rowing Club, you will find the Hyde Street Pier (open daily; 10:00 a.m. to 5:00 p.m., until 6:00 p.m. during the summer; small admission charge for adults). It boasts of being the largest collection of historic ships in the country.

Docked here are a century of sailing—from the Balclutha, which carried grain around Cape Horn, to the Eureka, a sidewheel ferryboat which carried commuters across the Bay before the Golden Gate Bridge was built.

And I recommend you board one of them—the Balclutha. But keep an eye on your watch; we have a full day planned.

The Balclutha is the last full-rigged ship of the great Cape Horn Fleet. It has been faithfully restored through the generosity of its sponsor, the San Francisco Maritime Museum Association, as well as through contributions from public-spirited San Franciscans, and by members of San Francisco unions who donated thousands of labor hours without charge.

Although the Balclutha is anchored permanently at the Hyde Street Pier, it is easy to imagine her anchor is aweigh and you are sailing off in freedom and glory on the world's trade routes for the romantic past of the Balclutha hangs to her from stem to stern.

Even the galley and captain's cabin have been restored accurately. If you have any youngsters in your party, looking over every part of this great ship will be certainly one of the highlights of your visit to San Francisco. And even if no children are present, who among us cannot be caught up in the magical daydream of casting off in a full-rigged sailing ship like the Balclutha?

After leaving the Hyde Street Pier, continue down Jefferson Street toward Fisherman's Wharf.

However, before arriving at the Wharf proper, you may wish to take a slight detour to The Cannery, a dramatic dining-shopping complex of unusual design. You can't miss it, for it is on the right-hand side of Jefferson Street as you approach Fisherman's Wharf.

If you are lucky enough to be here when the famous local San Francisco crabs are in season (usually mid-November to mid-May), you are in for a real treat. Crabs are served in San Francisco all year around but during the off-season, they come in iced from other areas.

The famous San Francisco crab is not to be confused with the smaller, soft-shelled crab of the East Coast. It is closer in flavor and size to the eastern lobster rather than to the eastern crab. The best way to enjoy our marvelous crab is freshly picked from the shell, sprinkled with lemon juice or dipped into a plain, good-quality mayonnaise, perhaps flavored with a dash of mustard.

One of the few San Francisco culinary habits I do not endorse is covering crab with something called Louis sauce, which overpowers the crab's delicate flavor. Louis dressing, by the way, seems to be nothing but a diabolic mixture of mayonnaise and catsup. And while at it, I should also like to veto the widespread practice of placing so-called cocktail sauce on San Francisco crab. That's more destructive than Louis!

Another seafood delicacy which you will find at the Wharf is the "tiny bay shrimp." Many years ago, San Francisco Bay was filled with delectable little crustaceans very similar to these and thus the name "bay shrimp."

However, man's pollution and the high cost of fishing for the few that remain in the Bay put an end to their being commercially fished locally. Therefore, just about all the "bay shrimp" you will find on the Wharf and in restaurants come from up and down the Pacific Coast and are shipped in iced.

By the way, since seafood terminology has never been universally standardized, most local restaurants reserve the term "shrimp" for these tiny crustaceans, and "prawns" for the larger ones. There are no local varieties of prawns; the vast majority of those you find in San Francisco are shipped in from the coast of Mexico or New Orleans, usually frozen. Oh, yes, while I strenuously object to the cocktail sauce on crab, I do enjoy it on shrimp. But even then I request it be served "on the side" in order that I may add just the right amount.

At this point, I might tell you about a feud I had with one of our famous local Italian restaurants. The owner insisted upon serving his shrimp cocktails with spoons rather than forks. When I objected, he told me there was too much sauce to use a fork. This, of course, was exactly my point! But plead as I might to use less sauce, he persisted and seems to be doing nicely without my patronage.

Your stroll along Fisherman's Wharf will also introduce you to another San Francisco culinary favorite—our famous sourdough bread. You will spot it either in a heavy, round dome or in a long, cylindrical baton like the traditional French bread loaf. The dome-like loaf has a very hard outer crust with a rather coarse texture inside; the long cylindrical loaf seems to have a softer crust and a smoother inner texture—both, of course, possess a slight sour taste.

Natives continually complain that the sourdough isn't as sour as it once was, which may be true. Nevertheless, it is still one of the world's greatest breads. Oh, if you fall in love with our sourdough and wish to take a "bite" of San Francisco home with you, you will find racks of them at the airport. But we had better be moving on along the Wharf right now.

At the water's edge near Pier 43 1/2, you will find your closest, land-based view of Alcatraz. If one of the world's most famous former prisons truly fascinates you (it holds no interest for me), you might want to visit the "Rock." However, reservations for your jaunt to Alcatraz Island, now part of the Golden Gate Recreation Area of the National Park Service, usually must be made in advance for a specific day and time. Sometimes, in the peak visitor season, there can be up to a three-week wait!

Therefore, it is best to reserve tickets in advance through Ticketron, Inc. by calling 392-SHOW. Oh yes, should you decide to visit Alcatraz at some time during your stay, be sure to wear warm clothing and sturdy walking shoes.

When you have seen enough of the Wharf area, you can take another cable car back to the downtown area. But you don't have to walk back to Hyde Street, instead walk three blocks up Taylor Street away from Fisherman's Wharf and you will find the terminal point of another cable car line, the Powell Street line.

11:45 a.m.   Board a cable car here, regardless of which restaurant you have chosen for lunch.

If you have decided on the Chinese dim sum lunch, get off at Pacific Avenue and walk downhill to Tung Fong, 808 Pacific Avenue (362-7115; open for lunch every day except Wednesday).

San Francisco has a vast assortment of dim sum restaurants, but this tiny hole-in-the-wall is regarded as one of the finest exponents of this intriguing Chinese luncheon tradition. While other huge dim sum emporiums, such as Asia Garden down the street and the Hong Kong across the street, may perhaps offer a greater variety of dishes, I give the edge on quality to little Tung Fong.

Dim sum, which translates as "heart's delights," are one of the great delights of Chinese cookery. They are little snacks which offer an exquisite array of textures and flavors. If you have never experienced a dim sum lunch, all you need to remember is to remain open-minded and adventuresome!

There is no set menu: what you do is hail a tray-laden waitress and select at random any of the stuffed dumplings, tiny sparerib sections, egg rolls, custard tarts, or whatever else happens to be on the tray. You will then be served a small plate containing two or three portions of each selection. There are no prices; your check will be tabulated by adding up the empty plates at the end of the meal.

Because prices are remarkably low, let yourself go. Be sure to include favorites such as chicken in foil; char sil bow (barbecued pork in a puffy steamed bun); fon gor (pink shrimp visible through the thin steamed-dough covering); and custard tart for your dessert—each sensational!

After your filling dim sum lunch, a walk through Chinatown before getting behind the wheel of your rented car or in the seat of a tour bus would feel just right. So proceed downhill to Grant Avenue, turn right, and you will find yourself in the heart of Chinatown—the world's largest Chinese community outside the Far East.

You are taking your stroll at the best time of day, too, for this is when the streets are packed with Chinese residents doing their marketing for the evening meal.

Because of the reliance of Chinese cuisine on the freshest ingredients, Chinese women shop daily in the afternoon. Thus, you will find the fish markets, delicatessens and green grocers jammed with shoppers—and I daresay you will be among them, for the aromas streaming out of Chinatown's markets are simply enticing! Street scenes in Hong Kong or Taipei are hardly more colorful or more fun!

Naturally, in between the food shops (the mainstay of Chinatown's residents) are the curio and gift stores. The quality of wares to be found here ranges from blatant junk to priceless antiques. During your Fourth Perfect Day, I will devote a whole morning to a walking tour of Chinatown, but right now it's just window-shopping and strolling as you head toward downtown San Francisco.

If you decided not to lunch at Tung Fong but rather at Postrio, remain on the cable car until it reaches Union Square. Get off there—Post Street—and turn right for a block and a half.

Postrio, 545 Post Street (776-7825; open daily for breakfast, lunch and dinner; reservations a must), is the San Francisco offspring of Wolfgang Puck, whose Spago has been Hollywood's star-studded "in" restaurant for years. But here he is aided and abetted by Anne and David Gingrass—thus the "trio" in the title.

Puck's creations can be as impish as his name, but with roots implanted firmly in classic French cuisine, he seldom ventures into the world of "dartboard cookery."

Dartboard cookery describes for me the bewildering output of some trendy kitchens, where obviously a blindfolded chef tosses several darts at a giant list of every imaginable ingredient. Where they hit is what he combines into dishes that have no rhyme nor reason. But while some of Postrio's dishes are daring, there is almost always an underlying rhyme to the reason. The result is a tantalizing, light style of cuisine which I find especially welcome at lunch.

As you arrive, you are welcomed at a street-level bar and then shown downstairs to the dining areas. I don't particularly like the mezzanine level with its rather low ceiling. But the main room is a winner. With an open kitchen, mammoth floral arrangements, wildly amusing pink chandeliers and a supposedly $1 million Rauschenberg mirror painting on the wall, it's big, open, comfortable, chic and totally unstuffy. During the week, it is an ideal setting for San Francisco's x-ray women, dieted to near transparency and breathless from shopping forays at Magnin's or Saks.

For starters, the thinly sliced smoked sturgeon is perfection, not too heavily smoked and served with horseradish cream and a salad of summer beans. A barley soup, piping hot and aromatic with fresh herbs, is ideal if your cable car ride was a mite chilly. While I find their smoked veal tortelloni somewhat heavier than their usual lighter-than-air fare, nevertheless, with a dark rosemaried tomato sauce, they are mighty intriguing.

The spicy curry risotto reveals a consummate understanding of how Italian rice should be cooked—ever so slightly underdone, creamy but not soupy. The curry, while authoritative, does not overwhelm the flavor of the roasted crab meat which has been incorporated into the rice. On top—slivers of roasted carrot. Superb! But then so is the grilled shrimp. Not even the slightest hint of the iodous flavor all too common in San Francisco, where 90% of the shrimp are frozen and mishandled. Sweet and pink, the shrimp are nestled upon a bed of finely diced vegetables, made creamy by avocado and touched with basil in the vinaigrette. The sauteed scallops are tiny and cooked until a lovely brown glow is raised on their pristine white cheeks. To set them off is a black olive, basil and olive oil vinaigrette on baby greens. So light, so right.

The pastry list used to be anxiety-inducing and I could never decide between the dozen or more choices! But

Postrio obliges by offering a sampler. Then you can pig out with the likes of caramel-macadamia nut tart, marjolaine with fresh raspberry sauce, an incredible chocolate mousse cake.

Yet, on the other hand, if they have a creation like their warm apple crumb pie with creme fraiche ice cream, be brave. Because in an individual pie tin will be the ultimate apple pie, not despoiled by too much sugar or cinnamon, and served with creme fraiche in ice cream form. How do those x-ray women stay so thin?

To help things merrily along there is an extensive and well-researched California wine list with some fine labels (like Edna Valley Chardonnay) available by the glass. Postrio is one of the hottest restaurants in town, deservedly so. And not all that expensive either.

Now, if the Garden Court was your luncheon selection, remain on the cable car until it reaches Market Street, its final destination. When you get off, turn left on Market Street toward the Ferry Building Tower (you will see it at the end of the street). Walk about four blocks and you will be at the Sheraton-Palace Hotel, Market at New Montgomery (392-8600; lunch served Monday through Friday), with its breathtaking Garden Court.

The Garden Court was once one of the city's proudest dining rooms and the hotel itself was called "the world's grandest hotel" at its opening in 1875. Luckily, we still have the Garden Court (preserved as a historical monument) to remind us what hotel architecture was like in that era of gracious spaciousness before the invention of plastic and neon. And should you be extra lucky in lunching there on a sunny day with the sun's rays streaming through the high, glassed ceiling, breaking into rainbow hues as they hit the prisms of the huge chandeliers, you might believe you are really back in the year 1875.

Culinarily, the opulent Garden Court has not been considered seriously for years. And I have no idea what will happen to its cuisine when the room reopens late in 1990. But it would be nice if it still featured a dish invented here—the Green Goddess salad.

"Green Goddess" was the name of a 1915 stage vehicle for actor George Arliss and it was the Palace's chef who invented this now nationally popular dressing as a tribute to the star. For over seventy years, the kitchen turned out a commendable version of this mayonnaise-anchovy-tarragon blend (emphasis on the last ingredient) which dressed the lettuce topped with your choice of shrimp, chicken or crab in the Green Goddess Salad. Let's hope they continue the tradition.

The Palace Hotel also has another room which you might enjoy seeing. The Pied Piper Room is right off the lobby near the Market street entrance. The claim to fame of this charming wood-panelled room is the huge Maxfield Parrish painting that spans the back of the bar.

2:00 p.m.   Now it's time to see more of the city. Assuming that your one perfect day in San Francisco will not be too restrained by a budget, I have advised a rather expensive item for this afternoon—renting a car. My reason is the 49-Mile Drive. This driving-tour of the city is a magnificent concept, especially for San Francisco with its incredible views. And the people who conceived the idea certainly deserve the undying gratitude of residents and visitors alike.

The drive is very simple, even if you have never set foot inside the city's limits before, because the route is well marked. All along the 49-mile course are seemingly hundreds of blue-and-white seagull signs indicating the necessary turns and directions.

Also, a complete map of the city with the drive clearly outlined is on sale at most bookstores and magazine stands, or available free of charge from the San Francisco Visitors & Convention Bureau Information Center, located in Hallidie Plaza adjacent to the cable car turntable at the foot of Powell and Market Streets (open daily from 9 a.m., except Sundays from 10 a.m.).

Because at times some of the 49-Mile Drive signs can be displaced due to road construction—or destroyed by vandals—I strongly recommend that you obtain this map before embarking on the drive. In addition, many of Golden Gate Park's roads are closed to automobile traffic on Sunday, and the Visitors Bureau map will show you an alternate route through the park. By the way, if you call the Visitors Bureau at a special number (391-2001), you will hear a recording of all important events in the city for that week.

Of course, if you would like to leave the driving to someone else, large comfortable chauffeur-driven limousines are available for less than what you might think from services such as Grosvenor Limousine Service (824-6767). And if you cannot rent a car or limousine, do not feel disappointed in substituting the Gray Line Tour No. 1 of the city which leaves around 2:30 p.m. (also at 3:30 during summer months) from their terminal at First and Mission Streets (558-9400). Passengers may also board at Union Square or even be picked up at major hotels. Check with Gray Line for details.

There will be a slight duplication on sights you have already seen this morning, such as Fisherman's Wharf, but certainly not enough to hamper your enjoyment. Since those taking either a limousine or the Gray Line Tour No. 1 will need no further assistance, I will now personally conduct the 49-Mile Drive. Just ask your car rental office how to find the Civic Center.

2:15 p.m. Start on Van Ness Avenue at the City Hall with its dome towering 308 feet above the street—over 16 feet higher than the Capitol in Washington, D.C.

Diagonally across Van Ness on the corner of Grove Street is the Louise M. Davies Symphony Hall. Opened with a nationally televised concert in 1980, this is now the home of the highly respected San Francisco Symphony. Even though it is graced by a large Henry Moore sculpture, its curved glass facade is often likened to that of a giant bus terminal. And even nastier things are said about the problematic acoustics inside.

Directly across Van Ness are twin buildings—the War Memorial Opera House and the Veteran's Building. Since its opening night performance on October 15, 1932 of *Tosca* with the legendary Claudia Muzio in the title role, the Opera House has been the hub of the city's cultural life and is the home of the San Francisco Opera and the San Francisco Ballet.

The Veteran's Building next door houses the Herbst Theater on its main floor, a lovely 1,000-seat concert hall, ideally suited for recitals. On its upper floors is the Museum of Modern Art with a permanent collection including Matisse, Picasso, Rivera, and others. However, now is not the time for museum-viewing—I've scheduled that later on in your stay. This afternoon, we just want to get a feeling of the entire city. So off you go up Van Ness Avenue, heading north.

At Geary Street, you will spot a 49-Mile Drive marker; turn left. Proceed along Geary, and in two blocks on your left you will see imposing St. Mary's Cathedral, seat of the Roman Catholic archdiocese of San Francisco. Many of the same wags to dub Davies Hall a bus station liken the design of St. Mary's to that of an agitator in an old-fashioned Maytag clothes washer.

Soon you will pass the Japanese Trade & Cultural Center on the right. Here you exit Geary on the right at the 49-Mile Drive sign. But instead of turning sharp right, as the marker indicates, drive directly ahead one block to Fillmore Street—then turn right. (If you followed the 49-Mile Drive sign, it would direct you back downtown, through Chinatown and Fisherman's Wharf, which you have seen.)

This section of Fillmore Street, with its wealth of interesting shops and restaurants is delightful to explore on foot. And if nearby Japantown does not interest (it is scheduled for your Fifth Day), you might substitute a stroll along Fillmore instead on that day.

Continue out Fillmore Street. Then just look at the view straight ahead as you plunge (use low gear) off the crest of Pacific Heights. You will notice that because of the steepness of the street, the sidewalks are actually stairs.

Right before you reach the Bay, the residential area on

your left is "The Marina", the area of San Francisco hardest hit by the October 17, 1989 earthquake. As I write these words, homes are still being demolished and reconstruction has not even begun yet. But I hope that by the time of your visit, the scars of that disaster will be healed and this lovely neighborhood will have returned to its peaceful norm.

When you reach the Bay's edge, Marina Boulevard, turn left for three blocks to Scott Street. Another left onto Scott places you back on the official 49-Mile Drive route, with its familiar blue-and-white seagull signs, leading you to the Palace of Fine Arts.

The Palace of Fine Arts, designed by Bernard Maybeck, derives its name from the role it played in the 1915 Panama-Pacific International Exposition when it housed the art exhibit. Today, it is the last remaining building of the Exposition.

Several years ago, when the Palace was about to fall apart from old age, Walter Johnson of San Francisco donated over $2 million toward its restoration, with the city and state also contributing. Proponents of modern architecture suggested the money be used to tear down the building. San Franciscans were aghast at such an idea, having long treasured the Palace as a symbol of a past era when buildings were created as a feast for the eye rather than solutions to economic and functional needs.

Thus, the Palace of Fine Arts is today as it was yesterday—that is, in outward appearance. Inside, there is a 20th-century museum called Exploratorium. The theme is perception, and there are over 200 exhibits which you can manipulate and activate to make you more aware of your perceptional powers. The Exploratorium (561-0360) is open Wednesday from 10:00 p.m. to 9:30 p.m.; Thursday through Sunday from 10:00 a.m. to 5:00 p.m.; closed Monday and Tuesday. If you have young children with you, the Exploratorium should not be missed. So plan a visit at a later day.

Next, you enter the Presidio, the largest military reservation within a city's limits in the United States. The date—1776—on the gate as you enter is not a mistake, because the Presidio served as military headquarters of the soldiers of Charles III of Spain in that year. Later, on your left, you will pass the Officers' Club which is the only, and therefore the oldest, remaining adobe building erected by the Spaniards in San Francisco. Throughout your drive in the Presidio, you will be favored by panoramic views of the Bay and the Golden Gate.

On your left, as you proceed, you will see the National Military Cemetery, significant in that no other cemetery lies within the city limits. Peter B. Kyne, an author, loved to tell the story of how the authorities dealt with his plan to be buried in this cemetery, because it was the only possible way he could be interred within the confines of the city he loved so much. Being a veteran, he went one day to chat with the Commanding Officer, to whom he confided his great desire. When he asked the Commanding Officer if he could reserve a plot, the latter merely glanced at Mr. Kyne and replied in gruff tones, "Mr. Kyne, first come, first served!"

After winding through the Presidio's tree-lined streets, which always remind me of some sleepy college campus of years ago, you will begin climbing up toward the Golden Gate Bridge. However, watch for a sign on the right indicating Fort Point, where you will take a slight detour.

Situated at the strategic entrance to San Francisco Bay, the massive brick and iron fort was constructed in 1853, using Fort Sumter as a rough model. Its huge structure is impressive and so are the views of the Bay, the city, and the underside of the Golden Gate Bridge high above you. Do not spend too much time snapping spectacular pictures, though, for there are many miles and equally impressive sights ahead. By the way, going at a fairly leisurely pace with several short stops, the 49-Mile Drive takes about four hours.

From Fort Point, retrace your route back up to the main road, turning right. An optional detour is a few yards beyond this turn which would take you to a parking area near the Golden Gate Bridge Toll Plaza. However, I suggest you press on and reserve that stop for a few days later when you go over the bridge.

Again, following the now familiar blue-and-white seagull signs, continue through the Presidio and on to Sea Cliff with its beautiful homes overlooking the entrance to the Bay.

Our drive takes us next to the Palace of the Legion of Honor, a museum which also serves as a memorial to California's dead of the First World War. There are museums throughout the world with superior collections but few, if any, with a more magnificent setting. You will certainly want to park here and spend a few moments looking at both the Palace itself and the panoramic view it commands.

Returning to the 49-Mile Drive route and proceeding along Geary Boulevard, you will soon find the historic Cliff House on your right—and directly before you, the vast panorama of the Pacific Ocean pounding upon miles of beach.

The site of the Cliff House has been the locale for a restaurant ever since 1863 because of its vantage point overlooking the beach and rocks below where sea lions make their home. However, the building which now stands there is certainly not the original. In fact, there have been many Cliff Houses—most of which have been lost to fires. One was even blasted from its foundations when, in 1887, a schooner loaded with 40 tons of dynamite was driven onto the bluff below and exploded.

Looking far off to your right, if it is an exceptionally clear day, you will be able to see the Farallon Islands. San Francisco's city limits actually extend 32 miles west into the ocean to include this cluster of islands.

Now, on down the Great Highway, past the San Francisco Zoo, circling Lake Merced and onto Sunset Boulevard (not to be confused with the neon-jungle street of Hollywood fame) to Golden Gate Park, turning right as you enter the park.

How can I characterize this stupendous municipal undertaking except to say that few cities in the world can claim a park within their limits as beautiful and natural, yet entirely man-made!

Today, your 49-Mile Drive will take you along most of the park's main drives just to give you a perspective of its beauty and space. However, Golden Gate Park deserves far more than this cursory look and tomorrow, we will devote a whole afternoon to some of its delights, although it would actually take several days to fully explore its wonders. So just relax and enjoy your drive.

After exiting the park, turn right up Stanyan Street...then right onto Parnassus Avenue, passing the huge University of California Medical School campus. Then on to Twin Peaks.

From its 910-foot summit, Twin Peaks offers you a vast almost 360 degree panorama, including a sensational view of San Francisco and the East Bay. On a clear day, it is one of the most spectacular city views in the world; if it is foggy, you'll just have to buy a postcard of the view back at your hotel.

As you drive down Twin Peaks Boulevard and Roosevelt Way, you will catch sight of every conceivable type of architecture in this popular view-conscious neighborhood. Many of the houses perch high atop stilt-like foundations, craning over the roofs of others for a better view.

Crossing Market Street, your next stop is Mission Dolores, founded by the Franciscan Fathers in 1776 with the historic church dating from 1782. After your visit to Mission Dolores, continue on up Dolores Street. Here you will see a wild assortment of San Franciscan Victorian houses—"Painted Ladies" as they are often called.

Some years ago it became the vogue to restore these lovely old residences, but I feel many have gone too far in the use of color, often picking out the ornate wood details in rainbow hues. Nevertheless, they are great fun to see and some are very handsome.

Eventually, a left turn onto Army Street will take you into the industrial section of the city and onto one of the freeway routes (Highway 280) back towards downtown.

From elevated Highway 280, you will see spread before

you the skyline of downtown San Francisco. It provides quite a grand finale for your tour. Leave the freeway at Fourth Street, and by following the 49-Mile Drive signs, you will soon pass along San Francisco's once-bustling Embarcadero waterfront and historic Ferry Building.

One of the biggest blights on the city's beauty is the overhead freeway above you, which gives a depressing feeling to what could be an inordinately beautiful waterfront.

Almost from the moment it was constructed there have been citizens' movements to tear down this civic blunder. However, as of this writing, because of severe damage it suffered in the '89 earthquake, there may be no choice but to tear it down. So, if the freeway still looms over your head as you drive past the Ferry Building, the efforts of both citizens and Mother Nature obviously have not succeeded.

Opposite the Ferry Building is a fine bricked and planted plaza with one of the town's most controversial landmarks, the Vaillancourt walk-thru fountain. Many hailed its construction as the ultimate in modern design, while others have derided its appearance as something left by a dog with square bowels. You be your own judge! Your route now takes you through the financial district and onto Market Street, where the 49-Mile Drive ends. Find the shortest route back to your hotel for a brief rest and freshening up before hitting the town again for cocktails.

7:00 p.m.   To watch it grow dark from the Top of the Mark has been a favorite San Francisco twilight pastime ever since the Mark Hopkins Hotel was built on its choice Nob Hill site. By this time, you should know where the Mark Hopkins Hotel is—you passed within a half block of it this morning on your cable car ride.

Even though many skyscraper hotels and office buildings now boast view restaurants and cocktail lounges on their uppermost floor, top honors still go to the Top of the Mark.

Before you select a table, do not hesitate to walk around

the room, sampling the 360-degree view of America's most beautiful city. My perennial choice of table is on the west side (to the right as you enter the room) facing the Golden Gate and the setting sun. The Top of the Mark is always crowded and a prime table may be difficult to find; however, you can enjoy some aspects of the view from almost any table.

8:00 p.m.   Leave the Mark Hopkins, cross California Street and enter the Hotel Fairmont, which boasts what is probably America's most famous hotel lobby since it was featured in the TV hit series, *Hotel*. Our Fairmont was TV's St. Gregory. Here you may wish to stop for another cocktail or simply stroll around.

The Fairmont was designed by the famous architect, Stanford White, and rebuilt in 1907 after the 1906 fire had almost completely destroyed the original structure. (You will note here that San Franciscans prefer to refer to the 1906 earthquake as "the fire" rather than the earthquake. This is to make it clear that most of the damage was done by the ensuing fire rather than by the earthquake itself. However, today the 1989 earthquake is *the* quake.) If you are interested in seeing some old photos of the hotel pre-'06 Fire and of its rebuilding, be sure to walk down the corridor to the tower. There is a fine display here.

Leaving the Fairmont, you will see the famous Pacific Union Club across the street. The club's great contribution to San Francisco lies in preserving the only remaining famous Nob Hill mansion, built in 1885 at a cost of over $1.5 million by James Flood who was one of the Bonanza Barons. Today, it stands as a fortress of Conservativism.

Walking past the Flood Mansion and Huntington Park, just across Taylor Street, you will find imposing and splendid Grace Cathedral. The site, contributed by the famous Crocker family, was once the location of their mansion. The Cathedral houses the first seat of the Protestant Episcopal Church in America.

If the days are long enough, you may wish to wander around the crest of Nob Hill where you will see breathtaking views in almost every direction. The Masonic Temple is here, too, with its surprising wall of "glass" which you can see by peering through the front doors. Although it looks like a huge stained-glass window, the wall is actually a mosaic fused between two sheets of transparent plastic.

8:30 p.m.   Selecting where to dine on the first evening in any strange city is always a major decision for me. And reaching my choice of recommendations for you has involved a great deal of soul, as well as palate, searching.

What I have come up with is three entirely different restaurants —each different in style of cuisine and in price. They are three of my personal favorites. And if I were given to that silly practice of appending stars to my restaurant recommendations, all three would receive the top rank even though a dinner for two at one could cost you less than a mid-priced bottle of wine in another.

Fleur de Lys, 777 Sutter Street (673-7779; dinner nightly except Sunday; reservations essential), has been an off-and-on favorite since it was taken over by Maurice Rouas twenty years ago. At that time he hired famed decorator Michael Taylor to create an enchanting room—a tentlike affair of French floral fabrics, interspaced with mirrors.

But if the decor remained basically the same—regulars threaten boycott on the mere mention of change—the cuisine has had its ups and downs. But with the arrival of super-chef Hubert Keller a few years ago, Fleur de Lys soared to new heights. And today, Fleur de Lys is generally regarded as one of the greatest restaurants in San Francisco—and I would add in the United States.

Keller is one of those rare culinary geniuses who create a cuisine based on classic precepts, but with sufficient personal inspiration to immediately brand it as his own. And while he presents plates that are stunningly beautiful, the food upon them is still warm. I get fed up with chefs who play with the food to such an extent that what is served might be a *Gourmet* cover candidate but is tepid and limp.

At Fleur de Lys there is an a la carte menu of about two dozen selections and an ever-changing, set five-course

"Prestige Menu." I heartily recommend it, since it gives you a beautifully balanced dinner of what Chef Hubert considers his finest offerings for that day. And besides if you wish to substitute something from the a la carte menu, there is seldom any problem.

After all this appetite-whetting what can you expect? Well, how about New York state fresh foie gras, shipped here raw and conjured into a silken terrine, layered with black pepper and herbs. Perfect fresh toast rounds are the accompaniment. Or a lobster and coconut-milk soup—its Thai-based origins of ginger and lemon grass seasonings still obvious but refined by a fine French hand. Then from Norway there is the most fragile of salmon slices enfolded in a downy corn pancake with golden caviar. Get the picture?

For a fish course, the sauteed sea bass lightly dusted in corn meal is beautifully firm. It naps upon a bed of pureed potatoes and is crowned with tri-colored roasted peppers. Another extremely impressive first course is the fresh lobster salmis, pieces of lobster in a rich Americaine-style sauce which holds a veritable garden of julienned fresh vegetables. For those who like the ineffable subtlety of a scallop mousse you could not improve on Keller's version, resting on a bed of fresh spinach and touched by a lemony sauce.

As a main course, the lamb chops can be spectacular! Somehow Keller enrobes them in a vegetable mousse before they are roasted to absolute perfection! (He provides the same treatment for veal tenderloins with equal success.) The venison, ranch-raised in New Zealand, may revel in such creativity as a mustardy sabayon, served on a red beet coulis. Accompaniments can range from pommes dauphine to lovely little spaetzl. In the fall, there may be a puree of pumpkin to brighten the palate and the plate. And with fans of crunchy snow peas, each dish is as much a treat for the eye as the palate.

And then, of course, there is dessert. Let Maurice talk you into a plate featuring a selection of sweets—ultimate ices, warm tartlets of what is currently fresh in the fruit markets, mousses, etc. etc. etc. The wine list is huge, impressive and naturally costly. However, the extremely knowledgeable staff will often guide you, for example, off an overpriced import to a lesser priced but better-buy Californian, such as a Silver Oak Cabernet or a Grgich Hills Chardonnay.

Expensive, of course. But not as much, as say, New York's Lutece. And by my estimation far superior. This is as 'grand' as grande cuisine gets!

Square One, 190 Pacific Avenue at Front Street (788-1110; dinner nightly; lunch served weekdays; reservations advised), is the creation of its chef-owner, the ever-present Joyce Goldstein, an alumna of Berkeley's famed Chez Panisse. The no-nonsense decor is not unlike an up-scale corporate cafeteria—blonde woods, unfrilly table settings, open kitchen. There is no doubt in anyone's mind that at Square One the food is the thing.

The daily-changing menu is an exciting eclectic gathering of worldwide dishes, with special emphasis on the Mediterranean area, often touched with the owner-chef's personal genius and daring.

For example, for starters you might find a fresh pasta combined with red onion rings, slices of pancetta, and slivers of sun-dried tomatoes, all of which have been lightly sauteed and then sprinkled with julienned raw basil leaves. By the way, the extremely accommodating servers will gladly split this and most pasta offerings, which tend to be generous in size.

A capacious bowl filled with a captivating carrot puree, spiked with French apple cider and a Calvados cream float is just one of Goldstein's many super soups. The house-baked breads, like the quintessential Italian wheat, are irresistible—ideal for sopping, dipping or just savoring with slabs of sweet butter.

If Ms. Goldstein is in a Moroccan mood, there might be a trio of North African salads—cumin-scented thinly sliced carrots, eggplant and a third of slightly underdone lentils, aromatic with mint.

While any chef can miscalculate, Ms. Goldstein seems incapable of error when it comes to dealing with pork. Her roast pork Florentine style, perfumed with rosemary, garlic and cloves is ideally moist and tender. For something more exotic, look for a West Indian pork ragout of onions, cloves, orange, nutmeg and rum, served with black beans and rice, steamed greens and fried bananas. A veritable carnival of flavors! If that's too complex, something simpler like her blushing-pink grilled baby lamb chops aided by a Bretonne white-bean ragout is simplicity and simply perfect.

Of course, all vegetables are always garden-fresh and superbly handled, such as grilled baby zucchini or brussels sprouts enriched by a cream sauce with pancetta and onions.

For dessert, a chocolate-pecan torte is featherweight and refreshingly semi-sweet; its moistening moat a maple-flavored creme anglaise. A coconut flan is accompanied by pineapple cubes marinated in dark rum. The summertime peach pie is down-home perfection: the winter fruit compote is a cinnamon-spiced stew of dried prunes and apricots. But my favorite Square One dessert is a sensually rich custard under a crunchy gingerbread crust served with heavy cream!

The wine list reflects the same care and understanding that makes Square One one of the city's finest restaurants. Upper-moderate price scale for luxury-class dining.

Golden Turtle, 2211 Van Ness Avenue near Broadway (441-4419; lunch and dinner daily except Monday; reservations advised). Today the cuisines of the Orient play leading roles in dining-out adventures in San Francisco. But that was not always the case.

Even though our Chinatown was established during the Gold Rush of the 19th century, in a 1940 guide book which listed over 120 restaurants, only ten were Chinese. All in Chinatown; all Cantonese. But after the Vietnam War, things changed dramatically. And now San Francisco restaurant-goers can compare not only the cuisines of the various provinces of China, but the national cuisines of just about every country in Southeast Asia in literally hundreds of restaurants.

We have restaurants specializing in the cooking of Cambodia, Laos, Burma, Thailand and even Singapore. And for the exciting cuisine of Vietnam, there is no finer exponent than the Golden Turtle.

If you are well versed in this delectable national cuisine, then I only need say that at the Golden Turtle you will find your favorite dishes handsomely fashioned from impeccable ingredients. If you are a novice, let me be your guide through the vivid flavors and intriguing texture contrasts that make the cuisine of Vietnam and the Golden Turtle so special.

Appetizers are a very strong suit in all Southeast Asian cuisines. And probably the signature dish of Vietnam menus is the imperial roll, which Golden Turtle does superbly. Not unlike a Chinese spring roll, a fine rice-paper casing is filled with a mixtures of minced pork, vegetables and crab meat or shrimp and then deep fried until crackly crisp. But since the Vietnamese love contrasts, both in flavor and texture, you place the imperial roll onto a lettuce leaf along with mint, pickled cucumber and fine rice noodles. Wrap it all up and enjoy! Not to be missed.

Another intriguing appetizer is the shrimp and pork salad roll. This time the casing of tranlucent rice noodle is steamed and holds within shreds of pork, thinly sliced shrimp, more of that vermicelli-fine noodle and lettuce. Served at room temperature, you dip the salad roll into a spicy sauce before savoring its myriad flavors and textures. The same cast of culinary characters are also featured in a tossed salad, dressed in a light vinaigrette studded with peanuts.

For main courses, beef appears in a couple of my favorite dishes. In imperial beef, it is encased in strips of pork and then grilled. As with the imperial rolls, you wrap these in lettuce also. In Lot beef, the meat is already wrapped in a slightly bitter, deep green leaf and then grilled.

Lemon grass is a popular herb in all Southeast Asia cuisines. And the Vietnamese love to use its hauntingly sweetish flavor to enhance chicken and prawns. In the lemon grass curried prawns, the prawns are treated to a coconut-milk curry sauce, filled with sweet white onions and several kinds of mushrooms. And if the chefs at Golden Turtle are masters at subtly flavoring their creations, they are also wizards at frying, as their royal chicken will demonstrate.

My beverage of choice for this cuisine—many of the dishes of which can be spicy—is beer. And that helps bring the total dining tab to a remarkably modest sum, considering the splendid cooking. In fact, when you consider the lovely ambience—this is no store-front joint, but a handsome dining room with intricately carved wood walls—the deft service and, of course, the award-winning cuisine, the Golden Turtle is one of San Francisco's great dining bargains!

11:00 p.m.   When the Fairmont Hotel announced that it would close its Venetian Room on January 1, 1990, it sounded the death knell for the last of the major "name rooms" in San Francisco. Where will Joel Grey, our own Carol Channing, Tony "Left-My-Heart-Here" Bennett and other old, familiar faces appear now? Perhaps by the time of your visit, San Francisco will have found a new home for them.

However, we do have some local entertainers who like some wines don't seem to travel. So if you can find Weslia Whitfield or Peter Mintun appearing anywhere in town, don't miss them.

Weslia Whitfield is a cabaret singer *par excellence*. If you love the songs of the 30's, composed by some of America's greatest—Hammerstein, Kern, Arlen, Porter, Gershwin—or if you are just tired of being screamed at by today's supposed vocalists, Weslia will win you. Her "A Kiss to Build a Dream On" or "Just for a Thrill" can mesmerize a packed room.

Peter Mintun is piano specialist of this same period of American music. I don't believe anyone has ever heard him play anything written after 1939. For years his keyboard artistry made the bar in the now defunct L'Etoile *the* late-night stop. As of this writing, he is performing right down the street at Masons Restaurant in the Fairmont Hotel. If he is performing there—or anywhere in town tonight—drop by for a nightcap.

Of course, San Francisco has a bevy of nightclubs, comedy clubs, discos, jazz joints, etc. But since they come and go so rapidly, I have never found it feasible to list them in these pages.

Right now, the hot area for the late night scene is SOMA—South of Market. Here, in what was once a predominantly gay night-club area, are clubs like The DNA Lounge and DV8 where punkish Madonna look-alikes and Yuppies appear oblivious to each other as the beat batters on.

But you can easily find out what is happening there and elsewhere by consulting what everyone refers to as the "pink section" of San Francisco's only Sunday newspaper, *The Examiner-Chronicle.*

2:00 a.m.   After the first edition of this guidebook appeared many years ago, my telephone rang about 2:05 a.m. The voice on the other end was that of an obviously inebriated woman. "Hi there," she slurred. "I love your guidebook and have been following your suggestions all day. But it's now two in the morning, all the places have closed and you have no more suggestions. What should I do?" I told her as gently as I could to go to bed, and the next day my phone number became unlisted.

However, for those of you still up, I have a couple of suggestions. San Francisco, even with its overblown wicked reputation, does close up pretty tight at 2:00 a.m., the official "last call for alcohol" hour. Years ago, there were all sorts of places you could go to hear great jazz and drink watered-down scotch out of cracked coffee cups. But they are all gone—or at least that's what my cabbie-spies tell me. And even if they weren't, I couldn't recommend them in print—otherwise they would be gone for sure!

So if you are still game, how about taking a cab or the

car, if you have it, and driving up Telegraph Hill to Coit Tower—the remarkable edifice fashioned after a fire-hose nozzle as a tribute to our fire fighters by Lillie Hitchcock Coit—for a good-night look at the lights of San Francisco below you?

Or if you are hungry again, you can go to a place known to all as the "Coca Cola" restaurant but is in reality named Yuet Lee, 1300 Stockton Street on the corner of Broadway (982-6020; open daily except Tuesday from 11 am to 3 am; reservations for six or more; no alcohol so bring your own beer or wine; no credit cards).

Here in this unassuming tiny restaurant with its multi-colored facade and big Cola Cola sign (thus giving it its moniker), you will find some of the finest, albeit simple Chinese seafood in San Francisco. For amenities, the formica-topped tables have paper napkin dispensers. For beverages, there is only tea or naturally Coca Cola.

Even though the emphasis is seafood, you might want to start off with their meat dumpling in broth. In a truly tasty stock you will find small dough-encased meat balls of a re-markably delicate flavor and light texture.

If they have fresh crab—and here they mean "live" crab—try the crab in ginger, onion and coriander. Another winner is the quickly boiled medium prawns—blushing pink shrimp still in their shells. Sweet and bereft of any other flavoring! When I asked of their origins, I was told they had been flown in from somewhere sounding like Salem! But, frankly I couldn't care less where they came from or how—they were superb. And then there are sauteed clams in quite possibly the lightest pepper and black bean sauce you will ever encounter. If dropping by at 2 a.m. is not in your plans, you can visit Yuet Lee for lunch when our walking tour of Chinatown takes you out this way on our Fourth Perfect Day schedule.

3:00 a.m.   Good Night!

I hope you've enjoyed the day. And if your plans provide for a longer stay in San Francisco, I shall now take you through the second day of your one perfect week. So read on.

Your Second Perfect Day Schedule

9:00 a.m. Breakfast at Sears'.

10:00 a.m. Shopping tour of downtown San Francisco.

12:00 noon Lunch at either a classy bistro right off Union Square or at Greens with its Golden Gate view.

1:30 p.m. Drive or take easily accessible public transportation to Golden Gate Park. Visit the Flower Conservatory, de Young Museum, the Asian Art Museum, the Aquarium and Planetarium, or just stroll.

4:00 p.m. Tea at the Japanese Garden.

4:30 p.m. Climb Strawberry Hill or feed the birds on the edge of Stow Lake.

5:30 p.m. Back to your hotel to freshen up for dinner or go directly to one of two outstanding spots near Golden Gate Park—celestial Cambodian cuisine at down-to-earth prices or my favorite friendly but fantastic Avenues haunt. Or visit the city's most renowned pan-China palace in colorful Ghirardelli Square.

8:30 p.m. An early evening can stretch into a late-night romp at one of two vastly different local pubs—the American birthplace of Irish Coffee or a rowdy sports saloon that jokingly warns tourists away.

The Second Day of Your
One Perfect Week in San Francisco

Even though shopping is not one of my favorite pastimes, I realize I am in a distinct minority. And for those who are "born to shop" as their bumper strips proclaim, San Francisco's Union Square area is up there with Fifth Avenue, Michigan Avenue and Rodeo Drive as one of the nation's four highest dollar volume shopping meccas. For here in a few square blocks, you can find not only some of the most famous names in San Francisco merchandising, but outposts of Paris, Milan, London, Dallas, Tokyo and you name it.

So for this morning, let me qive you a quick guided tour of the Union Square area. If you don't mind, I'll stay outside the stores. And, if you want to complete this tour before lunch, you should not tarry too long either.

Armed with as many credit cards as you can muster, let's get started. But first, we should be fortified with a good breakfast.

9:00 a.m.   Sears', 439 Powell Street near Post (986-1160; closed Monday and Tuesday; breakfast and lunch only), is a San Francisco institution—without question *the* most popular place with San Franciscans for breakfast. And there are many world travelers who will rush here for their first meal of a San Francisco stay, as quickly as others rush to the Top of the Mark for cocktails. Little wonder, for where in the world will you find your plate shimmering with 18 pancakes (small, thank goodness!) crowned with whipped butter and maple syrup? And along with them, you can order excellent ham, bacon, link sausages or the very special smoked country sausage patties made especially for Sears'.

Breakfast to many is the most important meal of the day.

Sears' meets the challenge with distinction. Begin with an all-fresh fruit bowl, one of those lush melons from the display, or a glass of freshly squeezed orange juice. Then proceed to the famous pancakes; or to eggs beautifully cooked accompanied with crispy hash browns; or to a distinctive French toast made from San Francisco's famous sourdough bread. Then split an order of their baked-on-the-premises coffee cake. That should hold you until lunch.

10:00 a.m.   Now then, on leaving Sears' you find yourself in a perfect strategic position for our morning shopping tour—which will have to be of the "window" variety because of the short time I have allocated for it. However, you might want to pick up some personal needs which you neglected to pack or a gift for someone back home. Union Square is certainly the place to find it. So we're off.

Simply turn right for a half block when you exit Sears' and you are at Post Street, the northern boundary of Union Square. The square got its name for being the locale of several pro-Union demonstrations held here on the eve of the Civil War in 1860. But the Victory Monument in the Square's center commemorates yet another war— honoring Commodore Dewey's victory in Manila Bay, during the Spanish-American War.

So much for history! Now cross Powell Street—the cable car slot beneath your feet—and you stand at the entrance of our first stop, Saks Fifth Avenue.

Saks Fifth Avenue: Opened in 1981, the interior is a masterpiece of design. Built around a central light well, crisscrossed by escalators, the store gives the shopper a feeling of openness and ease. Of course, the main attraction is the high-style merchandise, but I love the place just for its beautiful, elegant self.

Bullock and Jones: Facing Union Square further down Post Street is this handsome building, reminiscent of fine old British establishments, devoted exclusively to apparel for the older man or the conservative younger one. They have a superb collection of fine English shoes and an

Aquascutum of London section on the third floor, which also carries women's wear. Exiting Bullock and Jones, turn left down Post to Stockton Street, turning left again to smile at the charming Ruth Asawa fountain—with its intricate 41 bronze friezes detailing San Francisco scenes—on the steps of the Grand Hyatt Hotel.

The Tailored Man: At 324 Stockton, directly across from the Hyatt Hotel. In sharp contrast to nearby Bullock and Jones, this lively shop features the very latest men's styles, greatly influenced by European high fashions. And if you cannot find what you want, expert craftsmen will make a custom-tailored suit for you from a wide selection of imported fabrics.

Scheuer Linens: Immediately next door to the Tailored Man is this long-established and reliable shop. This is where countless San Francisco families obtain luxurious linens for dining room, bath and bedroom. Many imported items are available here and nowhere else.

Waterford/Wedgwood San Francisco: Drop in here for the fine china and crystal to place upon those exquisite Scheuer linens.

Alfred Dunhill, Ltd.:   On the corner of Post and Stockton is the local branch of this world-wide purveyor of cigars, pipe tobacco and leather goods. They also feature a nice selection of men's clothes.

Gump's: Just a few doors further down Post Street from Alfred Dunhill's you will find what is probably San Francisco's most internationally known shop, and for good reason. Although its early reputation was gained by its priceless jade collection and some of its merchandise is still on the expensive side, it has introduced many items of good taste at amazingly reasonable prices. It is one of the best gift shops in San Francisco and certainly a place which deserves your attention if you plan to take gifts home as a reminder of your trip. You should not miss the jade collection on the third floor, or the limited but fine collection of lithographs and paintings.

Elizabeth Arden: Should any women visitors require "touch-up's" during their stay, this branch of the international chain is conveniently found between Gump's and Eddie Bauer.

Eddie Bauer: Famed for its goose-down products—from outdoor wear to indoor comforters—this store also carries men and women's sportswear, as well as everything you need for that camping or fishing expedition.

Shreve & Co.:   Corner of Post and Grant. The Tiffany of the West Coast. Or perhaps it is true, as some San Franciscans maintain, that Tiffany's is the Shreve of the East Coast. Either way, this is for you if you love the beautiful in china, sterling and jewelry. The Shreve building also has an interesting history. Constructed just one month prior to the '06 Fire, it was one of the few buildings in the area to survive. Now let us cross Grant Avenue and turn left— toward the gates of Chinatown—for a half block.

Tiffany's: A very small version of the New York original, but you can easily spend just as much money here as you can there.

Banana Republic Travel and Safari Clothes: If you are going off to some exotic land or just like the loose, super-casual look of safari clothes, you will want to check out this now nationwide firm that began nearby in Mill Valley.

Malm Luggage: For over 100 years, the leading luggage and leather goods shop. Always on hand is one of the widest selections of functional, as well as beautiful French Luggage, made in California and sold in the nation's luxury stores. Malm also maintains a fine repair service, to which they can direct you in case of need.

Candy Jar: A must for chocoholics who may need a quick fix.

Tom Wing & Son: On the corner of Post and Grant is this fine purveyor of jade and oriental art objects.

A. Sulka & Co. and Mark Cross: Next door to Tom Wing on Post Street, you will find these two outposts of New York's Fifth Avenue.

Williams-Sonoma: Another national store that had its origins here in San Francisco. With "Serving serious cooks" as their motto, Williams-Sonoma offers just about anything and everything you can imagine—and even some things you can't—for the preparation and presentation of food. You might wish to ask that your name be placed on their mailing list to receive their excellent catalogue.

Polo/Ralph Lauren: Further down the street, on the corner of Post and Kearny, is an entire shop devoted to one of the biggest names in American men's fashion. Frankly, I've always preferred our native Levis to designer jeans.

The Crocker Galleria: Here is a mini-mall, three stories high, all covered over with a glass roof, which makes it ideal for rainy day strolling. Its wares are international in range—from Italy the trendy fashions of chic Gianni Versace; from England the fine shoes of Church's and the soaps and scents of Crabtree & Evelyn; from Belgium Godiva Chocolates. And don't overlook Card-ology, a small shop on the second level specializing in amusing and often risque greeting cards. By the way, the building you see on Sutter Street at the opposite end of the galleria is one of downtown's most famous. Built in 1917 by architect Willis Polk, it is known as "the world's first glass curtain-walled structure."

Now retrace your steps back up Post—but on the south side of the street—to Grant.

David Stephen: Here are the trendy threads of Zegna, Canali and Armani.

Brooks Brothers: On the southwest corner is the local branch of that staid old New York institution which has steadfastly avoided "trendiness" since it was established in 1818. In fact, Brooks' windows look as if they have not been changed since then, probably giving many devotees a warm feeling that old values never die.

Now instead of continuing on back up Post Street, turn down Grant Avenue toward Market Street, toward that building in the distance whose giant fans of glass on the top give it that Emerald City of Oz look. (Actually it is a Marriott Hotel, circa 1989.)

The San Francisco Giant's Dugout, 170 Grant Avenue: Strictly for baseball fans. Seats to Giant games and all manner of Giant fashion are at bat here. (If this shop should be vacant at the time of your visit, it's probably because the Giants are no longer a San Francisco team. As we go to press, owner Bob Lurie threatens to move his team, unless the city comes up with a new stadium. It's a big issue persumably for everyone but me. My one and only visit to Candlestick Park was over 30 years, the night of Willie McCovey's debut. I nearly froze and the cuisine could not be recommended!)

Paul Bauer: Displays fine china and crystal, many with German accents.

Exclusive Cutlery Shop: A long-time San Francisco establishment specializing in knives, scissors and anything and everything that cuts.

Crate and Barrel: Directly across Grant Avenue has a colorful upscale selection of imported housewares.

Now you can head up Maiden Lane (opposite Paul Bauer) toward Union Square. On the right hand side of the lane you will find. . .

Cartier: Although arched in black marble, this is just the back door, but it still leads you into one of the most famous jewelry stores around.

Edward Robison Co.: Right across the lane from Cartier you will find frisky puppies, canaries and even perhaps a monkey or two. Many, many years ago, the Robison family owned a foodstore near the waterfront. Sailors, who in those long-ago days were usually deprived of fresh food on their lengthy sea voyages, often came in and bartered exotic birds and other pets for fresh edibles. Soon, the Robisons saw more potential in parakeets than in groceries. Thus today, many generations later, Edward Robison Co. remains the town's leading pet shop.

Circle Gallery: Number 140 is definitely the most famous building in the lane. This brown brick structure with its small, tunnel-like entrance is the only store in San Francisco, and one of the few in the world, designed by Frank Lloyd Wright. Here in 1949 he used the same architectural principle—a circular ramp—which he later used in his design for the Guggenheim Museum in New York. It provides an ideal setting for the gallery's handsome paintings.

Laura Ashley: Another back door leads you into a happy world of lovely floral fabrics in dresses or in home design.

Chanel: The world's most famous perfume and the only name in fashion to inspire a musical—Coco.
    Continuing up Maiden Lane, you reach Union Square.

San Francisco Ticket Box Office: In Union Square directly opposite Maiden Lane, offers half-price, day-of-performance tickets to many shows. It also houses a Bass Ticket outlet, which provides tickets for a wide variety of events.
    Now turn left down Stockton Street.

Hermes: One of the exalted names in classic French fashions, especially known for gloves and handbags at exalted prices.

Gucci: The shop for those with the initial "G" or for those who do not mind carrying the designer's advertising all over their luggage, scarves and shoes.

North Beach Leather: Born in San Francisco's own North Beach this shop finally made its debut on "The Square" in 1987. And today, you will find its leather fashions all over America, as well as on Sloane Street in London.

Neiman-Marcus: For years it appeared as though the famed Texas institution would never come to Union Square. The site had been occupied for a century by the venerable City of Paris Department Store. When it ceased to be, there was a considerable movement to preserve the ancient building, primarily because of its huge rotunda, in which a giant Christmas tree was erected every December. Well, after endless law suits and delays, Neiman's finally obtained permission to demolish the building providing they would somehow incorporate the revered rotunda into the new building. That they did.

And here it is, a part of old San Francisco in a Texan outpost. Now if they would only do something about the ugly harlequin pattern on the facade! (By the way, on its upper level the restored rotunda houses a restaurant of the same name. And while it is a stunning place to lunch—situated directly under the huge, multi-colored 26,000-piece glass dome—the cuisine is problematic.)

I. Magnin and Company: Even with the arrival of Saks (1981) and Neiman-Marcus (1982) to Union Square, I. Magnin still reigns as the *grande dame* to San Franciscans. Its clean, white, elegant exterior is matched by the elegance within. But don't let its austerity put you off. Even those on a very limited budget can find many items in excellent taste. And although noted mostly as a women's apparel shop, its men's department and gourmet food section are well worth investigating.

Macy's: As an overall department store, Macy's is without any doubt the most popular in downtown San Francisco. Not only does it literally surround I. Magnin, but has an extension across Stockton Street which houses its enormous men's and children's departments. At Macy's there is something for everyone and at every price. If you are visiting San Francisco at Easter, do not miss the traditional spectacular flower display that fills their Stockton Street windows and interior!

By now, you are probably beat. And we have a long afternoon of walking ahead. So we will end our shopping tour of Union Square here and decide on lunch. But before we do, let me give you a few more stores in the vicinity, which you may wish to check out on your own later in your stay.

San Francisco Center (Market Street at the foot of Powell Street): Opened in 1988, this is a multi-story urban shopping mall. But by far its main attraction is today's most exciting name in merchandising—Nordstrom. Nordstrom's major claim to fame, to me at least, is not the merchandise it sells but how it sells it. Tales on how Nordstrom pampers its customers with service have become folklore to shoppers. Shoes that squeaked after months of wear were returned with no questions asked. Want a package gift wrapped? You are not sent off to stand in line at some service desk. The clerk will do all that for you. And when it is ready, he or she will even deliver it to you in another department so you won't have to waste a minute of precious shopping time waiting. This kind of old-fashioned service in an age of "sorry, this isn't my department" inefficiency has made Nordstrom hot.

But the question is—can its current celebrity be strong enough to attract sufficient shoppers to this mall located on Market Street across from the cable car turntable? During its opening days, there were headlines of million-dollar days, of long lines of shoppers waiting to ride the unique curved escalators to its third floor location. But today many of the shops in the two-story mall still remain unrented as many shoppers fill the enormous, brocade-lined express elevators to carry them directly to Nordstrom. Only time will tell.

FAO Schwarz, Stockton corner of O'Farrell: Few people know that the FAO stands for Frederick Augusto Otto, but just about everyone knows that FAO Schwarz stands for great toys for kids—of all ages.

Anthony's Shoe Repairing Shop, 54 Geary Street: Not only is this little shop known for top-quality shoe and handbag repairing while you wait, but also for its outstanding shoe-dye facilities. They will even mail their work anywhere in the country.

Wilkes Bashford, Ltd., 375 Sutter Street, between Stockton and Grant: That Mercedes stretch limo double-parked in front is probably that of the current rock-star rage, loading up on some of the town's trendiest threads. Here are some of tomorrow's fashions, which can be as mind-boggling as their price tags.

Pierre Deux, 532 Sutter: Here is a trove of treasures if you are decorating your *maison* in the French Provincial manner.

The Forgotten Woman, 550 Sutter: Just because a lady cannot slip into one of St. Laurent's slinkier numbers, there is no reason she should be forgotten in the world of fashion. And in this special shop she is not—in fact, here she reigns supreme!

Jeffrey Davies, 575 Sutter: I generally detest artificial flowers, but the silk beauties you will find here are breathtaking. Often customers smell them to make certain they are not real. Fantastic arrangements are shipped anywhere. An intriguing shop not to be missed.

12:00 noon.   After a morning of shopping, I am sure you are ready for lunch. For those who wish to remain in the Union Square area, I have a fine elegant French bistro. And for those who have a car and wish to venture further afield, I can recommend an outstanding vegetarian restaurant with a view. The latter is also conveniently located for our afternoon activities—a walking tour of Golden Gate Park.

Janot's, 44 Campton Place off Stockton Street (392-5373; open daily except Sunday for lunch and dinner; reservations advised), is an up-scale but cozy French bistro secreted down a narrow alley, the entrance of which is right opposite the Hyatt's Asawa fountain. The dining room is blond wood, brick and brass; the tables set in china of an art-deco pattern which echoes the flower print on the canopies overhead. It's all smart and snazzy. And the cuisine reflects this classy ambience.

Since it is a bistro, Janot's is almost compelled to serve an onion soup. And it's a really good one! The soup itself is sweetly robust, blanketed with the requisite stringy melted cheese gratinee.

Other hot openers are tender crumb-covered manila clams accompanied by an mild-mannered avocado mousse. While a cold opener could be a daily special such as a slice of coulibiac of salmon—the pink fish layered with a spinach mousse and one of mushrooms, all enclosed in a pastry crust and set upon a velvety basil sauce.

If you only wish a salad for a lighter lunch, Janot's offers several of today's hot-and-cold variety. For example, succulently underdone grilled quail enthroned upon fresh spinach leaves barely moistened by a light vinaigrette and peppered with crisp bacon crumbs.

For main courses, there is superbly sauteed baby calf's liver with bacon and onions, or meltingly tender sauteed veal medallions served with egg-rich noodles. Desserts, unfortunately, can provide more eye appeal than palate pleasure. But little matter after a delightful lunch like this in such a vivacious setting.

My alternate luncheon recommendation is best reached by car. And because it is so enormously popular, reservations here are a must—and they should be made as far in advance as possible. Failing to obtain a reservation, you can probably be seated without much of a wait (but in a rather uncomfortable quasi-cocktail area), if you arrive promptly when the doors open at 11:30 a.m. Are all these complications worth the effort? Yes! Because Greens is one of San Francisco's most unusual and exciting restaurants.

Greens, Building A, Fort Mason (771-6222; lunch and dinner served Tuesday through Saturday), is situated in a barn-like structure, formerly a warehouse in what was an army fort. The barrenness of the massive, high-ceilinged room makes for a rather high noise level. But there are compensations: one wall of windows affords a magnificent view of the Marina, Golden Gate and Marin headlands, provided the fog is not in!

Begin with one of the Greens' soups, regardless of what it is. The kitchen appears nigh infallible in conjuring up creations such as a velvety eggplant soup, enlivened by a soupcon of garlicky rouille. And even if you are on the strictest diet, don't dare miss out on Greens' sensational house-baked breads. Greens is owned and operated by The Zen Center, which also runs one of the city's finest bakeries, Tassajara, the provider of Greens' baked goods. The basket on your table will usually include three different varieties. Hopefully it will contain a peerless egg twist or their French country rye, a monumental bread.

For a main course, Greens usually offers a pasta dish, such as ideally *al dente* fettucine tossed with brocolli flowerettes, sun-dried tomatoes, pinenuts, olive oil, fresh herbs and plenty of garlic. Or try something like their tostados—corn tortillas with refried blackbean chili, guacamole, jack cheese, lettuce, tomatoes, creme fraiche and cilantro. It is served with a hauntingly zesty piquant salsa. A Gruyere-cumin tart is perfectly baked with a sauteed leek-and-cheese filling. And, if possible, try to have one of their salads, the greens of which probably were grown on the Zen Center's organic farm, Green Gulch, over there in Marin County.

But forgo a salad if it will interfere with your having a dessert, again from Tassajara's ovens. It might be the perfect pumpkin pie, a boysenberry-raspberry tart with a melt-in-your-mouth crust, or a luscious banana-walnut cake. Greens serves no hard liquor, but always presents a limited but select offering of some of California's most interesting wines, available either by the glass or bottle.

Oh, by the way, perhaps you did not notice it but the

above recommended lucullan lunch contained not a speck of meat, fowl or fish. You see, Greens is strictly vegetarian. And that makes it all the more remarkable. In terms of culinary acumen, I consider Greens' kitchen to be one of the finest in the city. And when you consider that they work within the restricting confines of unbreachable vegetarian rules, their virtuosity becomes all the more astonishing. Because of their wondrous ways with flavors and textures, I somehow never notice that my meal at Greens lacks meat and fish. And that is the highest compliment I can pay them!

If you can't fit Greens in today—or it can't fit you in!—reserve for later in the week. But don't miss it. (To reach Greens from downtown, drive out to Van Ness Avenue, turn right to Bay Street, left on Bay to Laguna, and right on Laguna to Marina Blvd. The entrance to the Fort Mason Center, where Greens is located, is at Marina Blvd. and Buchanan.)

1:30 p.m.   And now for an afternoon in the park—San Francisco's inimitable Golden Gate Park. The park can be easily reached by public transportation or by car. The only necessity one must take is comfortable shoes, since seeing and feeling the beauty of the park is best experienced on foot.

For those driving from Greens, turn right onto Marina Blvd. after exiting the fort. Continue along Marina for about five blocks to Divisadero Street, then left onto Divisadero. Divisadero will take you over the crest of Pacific Heights and through the Western Addition to Fell Street. Turn right on Fell, first bearing to the left and then to the right as you enter the park proper. This places you on John F. Kennedy Drive and, in a few seconds, you will come to our first stop, the Flower Conservatory which is on your right.

Now, let me allow those of you who had lunch downtown at Janot's and are coming by bus to catch up. To reach Golden Gate Park by bus, simply walk down Stockton Street to Market. Board either a Hayes #21 or

Fulton #5 bus which will eventually take you along Fulton Street, the northern boundary of the park.

Leave the bus at Arguello Street and enter the park, keeping to the right. Continue to John F. Kennedy Drive, then turn left and you will quickly find yourself in front of a huge, ornate greenhouse, the Flower Conservatory.

The Conservatory is the oldest and most charming building in the park. It is a copy of the famous Kew Gardens near London and was originally designed for the private estate of James Lick near San Jose. Mr. Lick died before he could add this dazzling building to his collection. When the executors of his estate placed the materials for sale, a group of San Francisco citizens donated the purchase price and offered the materials to the park for erection.

Professional botanists may be disappointed because the Conservatory's collection of flowers and plants is not comparable to the great ones the world. However, it does house a beautifully arranged and pleasing display.

Enhancing its tropical collection, which includes a pool filled with water lilies of great size, is the Conservatory's fine assortment of hybrid orchids. Plus, the exhibition room in the west wing is changed almost monthly, featuring the outstanding blooms of the season. Many San Franciscans make it a point to visit this room with each change. We are told that all of the plants shown in the Conservatory are grown in the park's own nursery and none is obtained from the outside.

As you leave the Conservatory to return to Kennedy Drive, you will want to stroll among the outdoor flower beds, where you will also note a special display which usually spells out words of greeting to visiting organizations or proclaims civic fund-drives. The Conservatory is one of the city's showpieces which draws as many residents as out-of-town visitors.

To leave the area in front of the Flower Conservatory, cross Kennedy Drive by taking the underpass walkway, which places you on the south side of the thoroughfare. Turn right on exiting the tunnel and continue along the

paved path marked "bike route." Soon you will find yourself in a small grove of giant ferns, enormous leafy plants
with an other-worldly quality to them.

Your walk also will take you past the entrance to the
John McLaren Memorial Rhododendron Dell, marked by a
small statue of the "creator" of Golden Gate Park. The dell
itself is a 20-acre triangle, devoted almost exclusively to
the park's most popular flower. If your visit to San Francisco happens to be around late April, you must allow
yourself a few minutes to investigate this incredible collection of hundreds of rainbow-hued varieties.

Continuing on past the entrance to the Rhododendron
Dell, you soon reach (on your left) the entrance to a large
complex of buildings, surrounding a music concourse with
a band shell at the far end. This is the hub of the park's indoor activities. Circling the music concourse you will find:

The M. H. de Young Memorial Museum (directly to your
right) which concentrates on American art from Colonial
times to the present, featuring masterworks by Gilbert
Stuart, John Singer Sargent and Thomas Eakins. British art
by Gainsborough, Reynolds and others, as well as original
Chippendale furniture is also on view in addition to the
traditional arts of Africa, Oceania and the Americas. (750-
3600; closed Monday and Tuesday.)

The Asian Art Museum: The Avery Brundage Collection
is a two-story wing of the de Young, although it operates
independently. The Brundage is one of the greatest collections of the art of oriental civilizations. I personally have
seen finer only in Taiwan. For anyone interested in blue-
and-white porcelains, jade and the other exquisite art
forms developed centuries ago in the Orient, this museum
is an absolute must! (668-6921; closed Monday and
Tuesday.)

California Academy of Sciences (directly across the concourse from the de Young) houses an aquarium, hall of sci-
ence, museum, and a planetarium. Most impressive, to me,
is the Steinhart Aquarium with its 14,000-plus living
aquatic habitants and its Fish Roundabout, the only aquarium of its kind in the Western Hemisphere. (751-7145 for

current attractions and times for special events; open daily.)

If today is blessed by San Francisco's typical benign sunshine and the idea of walking miles of museum corridors does not appeal to you as much as the sight and scent of newly cut grass and blossoming flowers, I will not blame you for by-passing these fine institutions for another visit on perhaps a more conducively foggy or rainy afternoon. However, we have allowed sufficient time in this area for at least a short visit, so you might use the time to rest your feet by sitting in front of a great master canvas at the de Young.

If you want to look at more in the museums, don't try to "crack" all of them in a single day. The human eye cannot take in that much. So be selective—perhaps just sample the Brundage or visit only one section of the American art at the de Young. Today, we want to simply get the feel of this great park. You can always come back tomorrow or even on your next trip. After all, the object with sightseeing anywhere in the world is not how much you can see, but how well you can see it. And if your interests lie in the tremendous wealth of art, history and all aspects of nature and mankind which these buildings offer, you owe it to yourself to schedule a return visit sometime later in your stay.

4:00 p.m. And now what would be more appropriate after viewing the wonders of nature in the Rhododendron Dell and the Flower Conservatory and the wonders of creative man in a museum, than to see them brought together in harmony in the magic of the Japanese Tea Garden.

Japanese garden designers, artisans of the highest order, have a unique way of working with nature. In densely populated Japan, where land is at a premium, these geniuses are able to convert the smallest spaces into miraculous retreats where one can contemplate nature. Unfortunately, the serenity of this Japanese tea garden can be upset by vast hordes of camera-toting visitors brought in by polluting buses.

Yet, since it is late in the afternoon, most of the buses have pushed on and you can wander at will through the little pathways which wind in and around such delicately refreshing beauties as golden carp swimming in still ponds or tall bushes forever moving in a quiet breeze which seems to be everywhere in this precious garden.

And, if you are lucky enough to be in San Francisco during the early spring (from the end of February through April) the blossoming trees make the Tea Garden even more magical. Well, no matter when you visit, you will want to savor more of its Japanese flavor by making a short stop at the little tea house. Only tea and a few Japanese cookies are available. And be certain to take all the leftover cookies with you; you will be needing the crumbs in a few minutes.

4:30 p.m.   Leave the Japanese Tea Garden through the main entrance and proceed to your right to the intersection. There turn right (the sign reads "To 19th Avenue"), but in a few yards, take the first path off to the right. Keep on the path as it soon curves to the left around a huge tree. Ahead you will see a flight of concrete stairs. Climb them and on reaching the top keep to your right as you walk along Stow Lake.

Stow Lake is the largest lake in the park, and presents a scene of natural beauty and of people enjoying nature. Along its perimeter, you will see young and middle-aged joggers puffing along, elderly people in conversation with "park acquaintances" with whom they probably have shared the same bench every sunny afternoon for years, and children squealing with glee as they feed the geese, ducks and other water fowl who make Stow Lake their home. Be a child for a moment, yourself, and offer the birds the crumbs from those Japanese cookies.

In the center of Stow Lake, you will see a small island called Strawberry Hill, accessible by two bridges. It is one of my favorite places in the entire city. To reach this wonderful spot, simply follow the edge of the lake until you reach the large bridge. On crossing the bridge, turn to your left to the base of Huntington Falls.

Huntington Falls are totally man-made. And so is the hill from which they cascade some 75 feet. But no matter how "unnatural" this scene really is, it is still lovely. Especially if you don't look too closely at those big boulders which line the course of the falls. They too are man-made, because stones of this size do not exist in Golden Gate Park, which was entirely man-made itself. But more about that later. Right now, if you are up to it, why don't we climb the stairs alongside the falls which will take us to the top of the hill?

Along the way are breathing spots, which afford wonderful panoramas of the city. The higher you climb, the more beautiful the vista. At the very top, it's marvelous. Off to the right is the mass of buildings which make up the University of California Medical Center. Then directly ahead are the twin spires and dome of St. Ignatius Church, the focal point of the University of San Francisco. Further in the background is the dark monolith of the Bank of America, my least favorite building in town! And seemingly next door is the Transamerica pyramid, the skyline's most distinctive skyscraper.

At the very top, no matter which way you turn another area of San Francisco presents itself. Also because it takes some effort to make the climb and because the hill itself seems to be a "secret place" for many locals, those who do come here appear to be extra friendly. Invariably you will be greeted by quiet hellos in recognition that you share their place.

If you do not think you want to make the effort to climb up, perhaps you can read about the park while you rest alongside the shore.

Unlike most city parks which were merely shaped out of existing woodlands, the entire area of Golden Gate Park used to be little more than sand dunes swept back from the Pacific Ocean beach, with no lakes and practically no vegetation. This great park, in all its apparent natural variety, was constructed out of 1000 acres of barren land. But do not think that everybody applauded the attempt. There were those who were skeptical and ridiculed the planners.

They doubted the possibility of growing trees and grass on hills of sand which were constantly changing shape under driving ocean winds. But the miracle was accomplished!

Under the direction of William Hammond Hall, Park Superintendent in 1871, the first control of the sand was begun. Small boys were paid to go into the hills and collect seeds from wild plants which could grow in sand and provide anchorage.

In 1890, John McLaren became head of the park and remained so right up until his death in 1943. So great was his fame and his equally great contribution to the development of the park as we know it today, that many books on San Francisco have erred in crediting him as sole creator of this park raised out of sand. Though the original concept of Golden Gate Park was not Mr. McLaren's, its creative growth and brilliant nurturing were, for 53 years, in his hands. And it is because of him that Golden Gate Park has no "Keep Off The Grass" signs. With the exception of newly seeded areas, every nook and cranny of the park is open to the public.

Because every bit of vegetation you see in Golden Gate Park had to be cultivated and brought in from elsewhere, the park today houses what is probably the largest variety of trees and plants from all over the world ever assembled in a city park. The only varieties missing are those which have defied all possible attempts at growth in this climate.

5:30 p.m.   Or whenever you can pull yourself away from this great, relaxing spot, it's time to head back to your hotel—or even directly to dinner, if your day-long walkathon has whetted your appetite. In fact, two of my favorite restaurants are within walking distance. But before I tell you about them, let me assist those who wish to return to the Union Square area, our point of origin this morning.

If you are using public transportation, all you need do is walk back to the cement stairs which had brought you up to the level of the lake. Descend them and turn to the left at the bottom. In a few minutes you will reach Kennedy

Drive. Cross it and enter the Rose Garden. Walk directly through the Rose Garden and you will exit on the corner of Fulton and Park Presidio. Cross Park Presidio and board a Fulton #5 bus which will take you back downtown to Market Street.

If you have driven to the park, simply retrace your steps back to your car, parked in front of the Flower Conservatory. Right behind the Conservatory, you can exit the park onto Arguello Boulevard; turn right onto Geary, and you are on your way back to Union Square.

NOTE: You will notice that throughout this book, you are given drive-yourself and bus transportation directions. However, you can certainly substitute taxis. San Francisco has many taxi cab companies, all charging the same rate. For the best service, my personal preferences are the De Soto Cab Company (673-1414) and Luxor Cabs (282-4141). Be forewarned, though, that cab fares in San Francisco are probably among the highest in the nation.

6:30 p.m.   As I said, two of this evening's dinner recommendations are within walking distance of Golden Gate Park, while the third is San Francisco's most famous Chinese restaurant off in Ghirardelli Square.

L'Avenue, 3854 Geary Blvd. corner of Third Avenue (386-1555; open daily for dinner only; reservations essential), is—at this moment—my favorite San Francisco restaurant. And for a multitude of reasons.

First of all the cuisine is superb! You would categorize it as California *nouvelle*. But unlike all too many of those kitchens, L'Avenue doesn't spend so much time fussing to create photo-perfect plates until what is on them is tepid. And they don't intimately combine ingredients that should never have been introduced. L'Avenue is well-considered, expertly prepared creative cooking. But there is a wonderfully refreshing casual feeling to it.

In addition, you can walk into L'Avenue—provided you have a reservation—in casual clothes, while at the next table former-Mayor Dianne Feinstein can be elegantly entertaining. And the dining room staff here is relaxed and friendly. Oh, they know their stuff—and can offer good wine suggestions, too!—but they don't act like acolytes at some arcane religious ceremony.

And finally there is a wholesome plain-wrapper "eat and enjoy!" atmosphere. Not too long ago, I took a visitor from New York to L'Avenue. It just so happens, he was the original publisher of this guide nearly thirty years ago.

As we sat down in the packed, noisy room, he said "Boy! The food must be great here. You certainly wouldn't come here for the atmosphere!" But after his first forkful of a typically splendid appetizer, he exclaimed, "Wow, they sure know how to cook here!"

Since L'Avenue's menu changes bi-monthly, and nightly specials augment that selection, you may never find the dishes I will describe. Pity. But there will be others, equally stellar, in their place.

There is invariably a foie gras appetizer. And invariably I order it. Because who could resist fresh duck liver from Sonoma, lovingly sauteed until it is buttery, placed upon seemingly minutes-old greens and kissed with a grapefruit and champagne vinaigrette? Or—hold tight—impeccable smoked salmon topped with three different caviars, served with a crispy potato pancake and creme fraiche.

L'Avenue soups are legendary. Late in the year, a puree of fall vegetables, made pastel orange by pumpkin, might put in an appearance. Or how about steamed clams in a corn chowder with a roasted pepper puree on top?

For main courses, in about ten selections the gamut of meats and fish is completely covered. Tender loin of lamb is roasted to pink perfection, moistened with a balsamic vinegar sauce, and accompanied by sauteed greens and corn relish. Or they might wrap a range-fed veal chop in pancetta, pan roast it, glazing it with an herb puree and Parmesan cheese. The fish might be John Dory in a regal champagne-tarragon sauce, with simple sauteed spinach and radicchio. Get the picture? Totally accomplished, creative cuisine without fuss.

What do you mean, you'll pass up on dessert? While I am a confessed chocoholic, I can kick my habit here by opting for any fruit or berry concoction. Because they always use only the finest and freshest and combine them into such glories as a fresh peach and blackberry cobbler with vanilla ice cream.

The wine list is considerate in price range and selection. And the bar, which opens at 5 p.m., also stocks some fine single malt Scotches, especially welcome if you walk over from the park a little before the 6 p.m. first seating. What more could anyone want in a restaurant?

By the way, if you are walking over from the park, just follow my directions on leaving by foot. But when you get to the corner of Fulton and Park Presidio, walk four blocks to Geary Blvd., turn right and walk (or take a bus) ten short blocks to L'Avenue. If you are driving, again take my directions for returning to Union Square, but instead of turning right on Geary Blvd., turn left for about three blocks. L'Avenue is right on the corner of Third Avenue and Geary, immediately next door to a vast sports bar, which proclaims on its green awning "We cheat tourists and drunks."

Angkor Wat, 4217 Geary Blvd. between 6th and 7th Avenues (221-7887; open nightly for dinner except Monday; reservations suggested), is only three blocks up Geary but culinarily it's like travelling clear across the Pacific. Like their neighbors, the Vietnamese, the Cambodians are charming, polite people. As you are shown to your table by a costumed hostess, scurrying waiters fly about speeding the just-off-the-fire dishes to the tables. But it's all done in a happy, friendly flurry; there is no sense of disorganization, as often encountered in an intensely Italian restaurant.

And when you are seated at your Western table—white linen, a single rose, forks and knives not chopsticks, wine glasses—you will discover that your order is brought to you by any member of the staff that happens to be passing the kitchen when it comes up. They see that you receive it hot, and the chefs have seen that it is delicious!

As with all cuisines of Southeast Asia, I order dishes for the table not for any specific person. And we all share.

To start, I highly recommend their unique shredded green papaya salad. This papaya is totally unlike what you may enjoy at breakfast. It's green, crunchy and not sweet. Julienned pieces are tossed with tiny cubes of sauteed pork and prawns in a fresh lemon dressing, scented with mint and spiked with hot red chile. Other winners are the finger-sized Cambodian spring rolls, smaller and more fragile than their Chinese cuisine-cousins. And unlike the Vietnamese versions, which you may have encountered at the Golden Turtle last night, you do not roll these in lettuce. Rather you enjoy them with slightly sweet pickled vegetables, dressed in garlic, fish sauce and sugar.

And don't miss out on a soup. The classic Southeast Asian lemongrass soup with jumbo prawns is just about my favorite version in town. Here the stock is not so palate-numbingly hot with chile that it obliterates the profusion of other flavors. If you wish a more mild-mannered soup, then order their sensational chicken cube soup, aromatic with red curry, fresh basil and tamarind and filled with pieces of chicken, cabbage, carrots, and pineapple with soothing coconut milk calming the intensity of the red chiles.

Like Vietnamese cuisine, that of Cambodia offers some intriguing barbecues. The charbroiled chicken is moist and succulent, its skin crisply charred and permeated with ginger and spices. An ideal foil for the crispiness of the chicken are the accompanying preserved vegetables, similar to Korea's kim chee, but not as overly "preserved." Beef rolls, which have been marinated in a ginger-garlic sauce are given the same treatment, but cooked on the rare side for perfect tenderness.

More Chinese in concept are some of the stir-fry dishes, such as a knock-out chicken sauteed with shredded ginger. Coriander, scallions, onions, cabbage are just some of the obvious ingredients that help light up your taste buds. But save room for their pan-fried catfish. Its skin is parchment crisp and darkened by a haunting semi-sweet glaze. Inside the fish is creamy textured and infinitely light.

The fried bananas, the popular finale, are somewhat overcome by a Grand Marnier sauce for my taste. But it's a minor flaw in an otherwise memorable evening of exciting dining—and at moderate prices. By the way, your evening at Angkor Wat can also include entertainment. On Friday and Saturday nights, a Cambodian dancer performs those beguilingly gentle movements on a stage in the farthest room. While charming, her performance does not compete with those in the kitchen who create Angkot Wat's dancing dishes!

My third dining choice for this evening is San Francisco's most renowned pan-Chinese restaurant: The Mandarin, located in Ghirardelli Square (673-8812: open daily for lunch and dinner; reservations advised), is far more than just another fine restaurant. It is the launchpad from which many of the diverse cuisines of China were sent rocketing into popularity across the nation. And it was all due to Mme. Cecilia Chiang.

Before Mme. Chiang opened her original Mandarin in a small cubbyhole far removed aesthetically and physically from this sumptuous site, San Francisco—and America, for that matter—knew little of Chinese cooking other than Cantonese. In fact, just about 99% of all Chinese restaurants in America were Cantonese.

I can still vividly recall my first taste of kung pao chicken at the original Mandarin some thirty years ago. Its shockingly spicy character was totally unlike any Chinese cuisine I had ever experienced.

Today, most metropolitan areas in America host hordes of restaurants devoted to the cuisines of Peking, Szechwan, Hunan and Shanghai. And in a vast number of those in the Bay Area you will find a Mandarin "graduate" in their kitchen. Yet, to me, The Mandarin still retains its unrivaled preeminence.

And the best way to enjoy its pan-China cuisine is to ask to speak to either Mme. Chiang or a knowledgeable maitre d'. Indicate that you are seriously interested in the finest in Chinese cuisine and wish assistance in planning your dinner.

Here is a favorite banquet of mine combining dishes from various regions of China. For openers, the chiao-tzu, those meat-filled steamed and then fried dumplings, are impeccable. And as a companion appetizer, the Mandarin squab is the finest I know. The richness of the finely minced squab contrasts perfectly with the cool flavor of the crisp lettuce cup in which it is presented.

The stuffed cucumber soup is an elegant dish—the cucumbers are filled with a forcemeat cooked in stock and then cut crosswise to reveal the stuffing.

The smoked tea duck with its dark skin looks somewhat like Peking duck, but it is totally different. This duck is eaten without any adornment, enabling you to fully savor the deep smoky flavor imparted by jasmine leaves.

For a taste of Shanghai cooking, try their shrimp, quickly wok sauteed with tiny fresh peas. A dulcet dish which works nicely in tandem with a bolder Szechwan offering.

If you are not familiar with fiery Szechwan cuisine, order their green beans in Szechwan sauce. It can make Tex-Mex chili seem cool in comparison.

There are also other dishes such as an exemplary mu shui pork, where shreds of omelette are mixed with pork and a myriad of vegetables. Then the mixture is placed onto pancakes which have been painted with a sweetish sauce. The waiter will demonstrate consummate skill as he rolls them using chopsticks. You eat these taco-like creations with your hands.

Or you could venture into Mongolia for their fire pot (advance notice required). In a chafing pot above a charcoal burner at your table, you will help create a marvelous dish of thinly sliced meat, chicken, fish, shrimp, bean curd and rice noodles by cooking them in a rich chicken stock.

The Mandarin also offers the only Chinese dessert I enjoy—banana sections glazed with in hot syrup which crystallizes when the bananas are dunked into ice water.

I can recall passing the kitchen of the original Mandarin

many, many years ago and seeing Danny Kaye feverishly working away helping prepare this very dessert. Danny was devoted to Chinese cookery—so much so that he created a restaurant-style Chinese kitchen in his Beverly Hills home. Like so many of us who are intrigued by unusual cuisines, he always loved The Mandarin and respected it for what it had done to introduce and promote the wonderfully diverse cuisines of China. And today, The Mandarin still offers the benchmark by which most of these dishes can be measured.

8:30 p.m.   After a full day of window shopping and park strolling, I can not imagine you would desire anything other than a comfortable hotel room right now. However, if you still feel like "going," and you are at The Mandarin, the Buena Vista Cafe is only a block away. And you might want to drop in before boarding your cable car to take you back downtown. Have an Irish Coffee for me!

If you dined at L'Avenue or Angkor Wat and you want a real look at local color, drop into the Mad Hatter Saloon next door to L'Avenue. There you can watch three TV sets simultaneously blaring different sports events to a cheering crowd. And be sure to cheer for the 49ers, Giants or Warriors in order not to give away the fact that you're a tourist. Remember what their sign says!

Oh yes, if you walked here from Golden Gate Park, any Geary Blvd. bus heading east will take you within a block of Union Square. See you tomorrow.

Your Third Perfect Day Schedule

9:00 a.m. While you are having your morning coffee, why don't you write some of those postcards?

10:00 a.m. Drive or take a bus to the Golden Gate Bridge for a short stroll on the world-famous span. It may no longer be the world's longest single span, but it certainly is the most beautiful!

10:45 a.m. Continue on, either by car or bus, to picturesque Sausalito with its dramatic view of San Francisco.

12:30 p.m. After a walk through Sausalito, lunch right on the water with a full view of the Bay, in the parlor of a former house of ill repute (no, not Sally Stanford's), in a ficus-forested locals' hangout or in an Italian trattoria.

2:00 p.m. Off to marvelous Muir Woods, natural habitat of our famed giant redwoods.

4:00 p.m. Time to drive back across the Golden Gate. If you took a bus over, you can now return via ferry and enjoy a cocktail on deck as it carries you back across the Bay.

6:00 p.m. Return to your hotel for a breather or dine early at San Francisco's oldest and most popular fish house.

8:00 p.m. If you didn't have an early dinner, you can now choose between a great Caesar salad with super steak or tantalizing Thai creations.

10:00 p.m. For laughs try one of our many comedy clubs. Who knows, Robin Williams might be on.

The Third Day of Your One Perfect Week in San Francisco

9:00 a.m.   If today is not a Monday, our plans are to leave town. This delightful little trip will enable you to see at very close hand the Golden Gate Bridge (in fact, you will cross it), the unique hillside town of Sausalito with its intriguing shops (many of which close on Mondays) and sweeping panorama of San Francisco, plus the giant redwood trees of Muir Woods. It's a trip you can make by car or a combination of bus, taxi and ferry boat. So have just a light breakfast at your hotel. And it's as good a time as any to write a couple of those promised post cards.

10:00 a.m.   Breakfast over, let's begin our trip. First, let me give directions for those wishing to drive. Find Franklin Street (it runs parallel to Van Ness). On Franklin (here I assume you are staying in the downtown area) turn right. Actually, you have to, since Franklin is one way!

As you proceed down Franklin, you will pass a few choice examples of Victorian homes, such as the Haas-Lilienthal House at number 2007 on your left. Built in 1886 in the Queen Anne style, it survived the '06 fire and is now open as a museum (call 441-3004 for tour information, if you are interested in seeing its interior). Another beautiful example—in the Italianate style—is on the far right corner of Franklin and Pacific. When you reach Lombard Street, turn left and proceed to the bridge, turning right into the "View Area" immediately prior to the toll plaza.

The Golden Gate Bridge was, for many years, known as the longest single-span suspension bridge in the world—4,200 feet between its towers. However, its length is not the chief reason for its fame. Other cities may build larger bridges or taller ones, but I doubt if they will ever build a more beautiful one. For to do so, they would have to match the setting—the beautiful coastlines on both sides, the majestic hills of Marin on the north, the city of San Francisco sparkling like a jewel on the south. They would have to build a machine to create great billowy banks of fog for stunning visual effects. They would have to make certain their calculations produce a graceful, simple and noble shape. And then they would have to paint their bridge red, a daring move which is usually a surprise to visitors who see it for the first time.

And so, if the Golden Gate Bridge has lost its title as the longest single-span suspension bridge in the world, it has not lost first place for grandeur and beauty.

Incidentally, if you simply must have statistics, here they are: The Golden Gate Bridge was first opened to pedestrian traffic on May 27, 1937, when 202,000 people thronged across it. The next day, vehicular traffic began.

On the 50th anniversary of its opening, it was decided to again ban automobiles from the bridge so that pedestrians could enjoy it in a giant Golden Anniversary walk-across. It sounded like a great idea.

But after a long debate—some argued for a full-day auto ban, while others said that would paralyze commerce and crucial traffic from Marin County—it was decided that from 7 a.m. to 9 a.m. on a May Sunday, only foot traffic would be allowed. At those hours, how many people could you expect? Ten thousand? Fifty thousand?

Well, San Franciscans outdid themselves—and almost did themselves in! For on that morning, over 333,000 men, women, and children—including the author and editor of these pages—tried to wedge themselves onto their beloved Golden Gate.

For those trapped mid-span for hours, unable to move, it was living hell. I even saw some brave souls climb over the railing and walk along the outer painters' platform in order to escape the crush.

Could the bridge have collapsed? No one rightly knows. But I know that when I saw after-the-fact pictures on how that concave arch became convex under the tremendous weight, I got goose bumps!

To this day, people still recount stories of their day on the bridge almost as frequently as those of their whereabouts during the '89 earthquake. But one good thing did come out of this celebration: the bridge's massive towers were night-lighted for the first time. And the effect was so beautiful, that the lights stayed. And we still enjoy them whenever we cross the bridge at night—provided the fog isn't in!

The bridge is 8,940 feet long and its pillars tower 746 feet above high tide. At the center, you find yourself 220 feet above low water which explains its attraction to suicides. The tops of the towers rise above the water approximately the same height as a 65-story building. But there are no statistics for the hours of pleasure it has provided both visitors who gasp at its breathtaking beauty upon first seeing it, and residents who cross it twice a day but never seem to tire of its beauty.

If there are children in your party, you now have an excellent chance to enjoy one of the delights of San Francisco while at the same time help your youngsters blow off steam—you can walk across the Golden Gate Bridge to the view area on the Marin County side.

(NOTE: If your party is split between the younger and older generations, part of your group may wish to drive the car across, meeting the walking contingent at the lookout point on the other side. However, please be warned that it is a long walk and you are not advised to attempt it unless you are dressed warmly and have a good deal of stamina.)

10:45 a.m.   After taking your fill of the sweep and majesty of this awe-inspiring structure and the fresh ocean breeze in your lungs, it is time to proceed to our next destination—Sausalito. Simply drive across the span and take the Alexander Avenue exit to the right.

The long downward drive from the highway into Sausalito is a beautiful one. On one side are the grass-covered, rolling hills of Marin, seemingly far removed from urban life; while on the other, you can catch glimpses of the towers of downtown San Francisco. A "Slow to 15" sign alerts you to the fact you are entering Sausalito.

And slowing down here is a good idea for it will also enable you to view the variety of houses perched on the hills above you. Up there, real estate prices are as spectacular as their picture-window views. (Average price of a Sausalito house in 1989 was $570,000.)

Proceed along the main street, which turns right, right again, then left along the water's edge. Immediately after the town square, another right turn will take you to a public parking lot. Along the way, if you do find street parking, fine. But be warned that Sausalito has diligent metermaids. And now let me escort those coming over by bus.

If you are making the trip by bus, find Van Ness Avenue. On Van Ness you will find several stops of the Golden Gate Transit line (call 332-6600 for schedule information). Their stops are marked by green, red and blue signs. You will find them on the corners of Van Ness and Geary, Sutter, Clay and Union. (Note: The Golden Gate Transit buses are not part of the San Francisco Municipal bus system, so you should be looking for the ones which are predominantly white and green, bearing the same tri-color insignia as the bus stop sign.) On boarding the bus, ask the driver to let you off at the Golden Gate Bridge toll plaza so you can view the bridge as did those going by car.

If you wish to walk across the span, you can do so and pick up a bus to Sausalito on the other side. However, because of the location of the bus stop on the Marin County side, you will be walking a good two miles.

Should you not wish to make this trek, after walking a ways out on the bridge, simply return to the spot where you got off and catch the next bus for Sausalito, disembarking at the main bus stop near the town square.

Now that we are all gathered here, let us start a short walking tour along Bridgeway, the main throughfare, back toward San Francisco, visible in the distance.

As you walk along the Bay's lapping edge, that rock in

the water which resembles a sea lion is not, of course, a natural phenomenon shaped by the sea into a likeness of the animal—but rather a stone carving. And one of the town's most amusing posters is a photo of an actual seal posing jubilantly atop his stone likeness.

At just about this point, a glance up the hill on your left will reveal a house looking somewhat like the truncated foundation for a fortress. Had not the indignation of some townspeople been brought to bear upon William Randolph Hearst, Sr., the building might have been completed and Sausalito could very well have been the possessor of a famed castle similar to San Simeon. But Mr. Hearst was invited to leave town by a delegation of husbands and fathers at the insistence of their wives who disapproved of Mr. Hearst's moral standards.

A little further along, Bridgeway ends but you can continue for another another block to the Chart House Restaurant, once the famed Valhalla restaurant, operated until her death by Sally Stanford, one of Sausalito's great characters.

Thousands of words have been written and a couple of films made about Sally Stanford and her unique checkered career. Years ago—World War II days—the name Sally Stanford was synonymous with San Francisco's shady nightlife; she was the proud madam of the town's most elegant bordello.

Later, Sally went "legit," and opened the Valhalla in Sausalito. Probably as a tongue-in-cheek reminder of her past, a red light always burned in an upstairs window. Then, in 1975, Sally Stanford achieved what she had been trying to do for many years—she became mayor of Sausalito. I like to think that Sally and her career could only have happened in places like San Francisco and Sausalito.

As you return toward the town square, the lefthand side of Bridgeway offers a bevy of shops, cluttered with the latest fashion, handcrafted jewelry and the most unusual in antiques.

Soon you will be back to town square with its two unusual and somewhat incongruous elephant statues to greet you. These elephants and that nearby fountain were originally part of the Panama-Pacific International Exposition held in San Francisco in 1915, and were donated to the city of Sausalito after the close of the Exposition.

Almost across the street is the Village Fair, a "must-see" for any visitor. The structure was an abandoned garage until it was converted into a showcase for several independent little shops. It is sort of a mini-Ghirardelli Square, although many years older. The Village Fair shopping complex was a natural for Sausalito, since the town was long famous for its local craftsmen and artisans. It is a delightful maze and don't hurry through—there are many things to see and buy.

12:30 p.m. Well, now it's time for lunch. But I must confess that during the thirty-some years I have lived in this heavenly town, it has never boasted a truly great restaurant. Well, perhaps the now-departed Ondine was "great" in its beginnings.

But right now there are several perfectly fine places for lunch. And the Casa Madrona, 801 Bridgeway (331-5888; open for lunch Monday through Friday; dinner nightly; reservations advised), is far and away my first choice.

After you enter the Casa Madrona Hotel on Bridgeway, you take an elevator to an upper floor, walk up two flights of stairs through a charming flower garden and enter what was once an old bordello. The comfortable cheery dining room retains some of the Victorian charm of its past. But the main focus is on the lovely view of Belvedere and Angel Island, with a small point of San Francisco visible from the glassed-in terrace.

The main part of the dining room is an especially nostalgic spot for me. For it was here that my career as restaurant critic was launched and a previously unknown area of consumer-oriented journalism created.

You see, back in 1967, restaurant criticism *per se* did not exist. For years, there had been restaurant ratings, as those published by France's Michelin Tire Company to encourage people to use their product by driving out to restaurants in the country. And of course there were puff-piece articles on dining out, penned by restaurant *writers*, such as gourmand Lucius Beebe. But seldom did a harsh word about a restaurant ever see printer's ink.

Therefore, when my partner Jack Shelton and I decided to create a monthly restaurant guide, in which we would present our unbiased findings after anonymously visiting restaurants, we were—like Abner Doubleday—inventing a game that had never previously been played.

Thus, not only did our *Private Guide to Restaurants* become America's first and most successful publication devoted to restaurant reviews, but it also spawned a type of journalism that is now practiced in magazines and newspapers throughout the country.

Anyhow, in the ensuing twenty-three years, this room has changed quite a bit and happily the cuisine even more so.

The menu at lunch currently consists mainly of rather light dishes, with emphasis on a set lunch menu of under 500 calories for under $15. And considering the flair with which they are composed, it is quite a bargain. For example, on a recent visit one such lunch began with a salad of warm, thinly sliced grilled eggplant set upon a bed of watercress and shredded endive—light, subtle and lovely.

The grilled seafood skewers—salmon, sea bass, mahi mahi—were superbly handled in a very light, fresh tomato sauce, all covering a small amount of excellent pasta. Dessert on this light lunch was a sensational pineapple-mint sorbet. I could hardly believe the claim that the entire affair added up to a mere 500 calores. And the equally meager price tag was an added attraction.

The remainder of the menu features such well-fashioned dishes as a broccoli soup—not cream thickened but creamy, with a novel tamarind cream on top. Truly excellent.

The Casa cioppino turned out to be an outstanding unthickened but rich, saffron-scented, fresh tomato stock filled with shreds of crab, some mussels, clams and pieces of fish. The garlicked toast on top was made from their own baked-on-the-premises, wonderfully dense bread.

For dessert, the expresso-flavored creme brulee, nicely finished to order, was not a true cream but closer to a coffee custard. On this visit, a Neyers Chardonnay was available by the glass. A lovely lunch, well served in a beautiful hillside aerie. And a bargain to boot. (The Casa Madrona is located about a half block north of the town square on Bridgeway.)

Horizons, 558 Bridgeway (331-3232; open daily for lunch and dinner), claims our attention primarily for its beautiful situation, just a few feet above the lapping waters of San Francisco Bay.

From its outdoor deck, you can watch the seagulls perform with the sweeping skyline of San Francisco as their backdrop. However, should the weather be too chilly, with dense fog not only grounding the birds but blotting out the spectacular view, you can lunch indoors in the midst of a forest of hanging ferns and highly polished wood.

The food will be serviceable. The somewhat spicier-than-most guacamole is pleasant, not the oft-encountered overmashed mush but textured with avocado chunks. But the tortilla chips are mundanely commerical.

Best bet for a main course is usually a fresh fish in season, such as petrale sole or salmon with adequately-handled fresh vegetables. The hamburger is of healthy size and is preceded by a pleasant small salad. More complicated cooking can prove to be somewhat chancy. A mud pie, made with Haagen-Dazs' superb coffee ice cream, is about the extent of the kitchen's creativity in that department. But that view—one of the greatest in the world—is far and away the most exciting aspect on this Horizon.

Angelino, 621 Bridgeway (331-5225; open daily for lunch and dinner), is the restaurant I frequent most often in Sausalito. But my judgement may be somewhat askew. You see it reminds me the most of *bella Italia* with its honest-to-God Italian atmosphere. There is Sal, the seemingly perpetually grouchy bartender. Then there are the waiters, properly Italian frantic, even when the place is deserted on a rainy January night. But who always have time to cry out "Ciao, Bello" or "Bella", as the case may be, to regulars as they leave. Also, there is a street-level view of San Francisco from a couple of tables.

But the thing that brings me to Angelino almost monthly is their linguine with fresh clams. I adore this dish. Yet, many versions—even those encountered in Italy—may suffer the cardinal sin of overcooked pasta. And the crime that damns any chef eternally to the lowest level of Dante's *Inferno*—canned clams. Some places even try to disguise the canned clams by placing a few fresh ones around the plate. *Vergogna*!

Not to worry. At Angelino the clams—as many as 42!—are all fresh and in their shells, mounded upon just-cooked *al dente* linguine. They have been flavored with plenty of garlic, some parsley and good olive oil. Ah!

But actually there are other fine dishes at Angelino. Somehow they manage to find the sweetest melon and the finest prosciutto for that favorite appetizer. And their calamari vinaigrette is also a winner—julienned strips of squid tossed with some preserved Italian vegetables. Their gnocchi is also fine and if you have gotten a cold from our wind-fog combo, I would suggest the tortellini in brodo. It's like being in Italy with San Francisco in the distance.

Marina's Bar and Grill, 305 Harbor Drive (332-0535; lunch and dinner daily), is a great hangout for locals who lunch there in a sunlight-filled room forested in ficus. One reason is that Marina's is not in the tourist area of town, but located a few blocks off Bridgeway at the north end of town, near our local supermarket and post office. Another reason is that its menu is nicely composed of an eclectic mixture of dishes—some all-American, some Asian, some south-of-the-border.

For example, the New England clam chowder is always tasty and filled with clams. The spinach salad never has less than the finest fresh leaves and the grilled sesame-seeded chicken breast on top is adequately moist. The burgers are big; the tender barbecued pork arrives on a hot-sauce soaked poppy-seed bun. The steamed manila clams are expertly flavored with tomatoes, garlic, white wine and cilantro.

Those are their regular mainstays. But take a glance at the daily specials. There are usually a couple varieties of fresh oysters and some finely-honed Asian-accented plates, like fish with a hunan sauce and delectable oriental-flavored stir-fried vegetables.

For dessert, when was the last time you had a real hot-fudge sundae? That's what Marina's is like. Good food, nice atmosphere—no more no less.

So with those four recommendations, the decision on where to lunch is entirely yours. Let your taste in food, your pocketbook and the weather be your guides.

2:00 p.m. O.K. time to go. It's off to the Muir Woods National Monument.

Again, allow me to give directions to those going by car. On leaving your parking space, drive through the town heading north. If you are going in the right direction, the mountain top you see ahead of you is Mount Tamalpais (2604 feet). Muir Woods is located at the bottom of its southern slope.

As you are exiting Sausalito, follow the sign indicating "Highway 101—Eureka". But stay in the far right lane and take the first turnoff which is marked "Mill Valley, Stinson Beach, Route 1." Follow the Route 1 signs as the road soon begins to cut through eucalyptus groves and curves over the rolling hillside.

When you reach the top of a grass-covered rise, there are some wonderful views of San Francisco Bay on the right. You will leave Route 1 at a turn-off marked "Muir Woods, 3 miles."

If you do not have a car, there are other means by which you can reach Muir Woods. Many tour companies—using those smaller more personal vans, since huge buses have been banned from these narrow roads—run daily tours from San Francisco to the woods, passing through Sausalito.

However, if you want to be more foot-loose and dictate

your own time schedule, you can easily take a taxi to the woods from Sausalito. It's not all that expensive, especially if there are four or five in your party. The Sausalito Yellow Cab Company (332-2200) does run a special taxi service to the woods. The fare is about $50 for up to five persons, and includes the round-trip cab ride along with approximately 40 minutes at the park. But whether you go by tour bus, by automobile or by taxi, you simply must go to Muir Woods.

Named in honor of famed naturalist-conservationist-writer John Muir, Muir Woods is the closest refuge to San Francisco of the giant sequoia, the redwood—the world's tallest living thing. Every great city has its so-called tourist attractions. These are usually termed "must sees." In fact, I myself used that term a few pages back. However, Muir Woods is not just a "must see," it is a "must experience!"

Frankly, I don't imagine many San Francisco residents spend a morning or afternoon going through Muir Woods on their own. Yet, it is amazing how eagerly they will volunteer to show visitors this beautiful park. Like residents of all cities, I guess we feel somewhat self-conscious about frequenting sightseeing spots. But just provide the excuse and I, for one, would be glad to spend many quiet hours in Muir Woods.

Naturally, the main attraction is the redwood tree, that unbelievably tall and majestic creation of nature. Although not the largest in the West, the ones which you are looking at rise an impressive 250 feet or more and reach a diameter of 17 feet. To see these trees would be reward enough, particularly at a point so close to the city of San Francisco. But Muir Woods offers more than this. It offers a natural habitat for the redwood—an exquisite environment of surrounding companion shrubs and wild flowers which have remained faithful to these great trees for centuries.

Take time to walk back into the woods a ways. You will be surprised how quickly you can detach yourself from the hub-bub of an arriving busload, most of whom head straight for the gift shop.

Walk back along the trail and find yourself a rippling brook and listen to its mellow sound for a while. Here, to me, the towering trees impact a cathedral aura, and the silence evokes a religious appreciation for life. If you want to ponder the insignificance of man, just sit quietly and consider the fact that some of these trees were already alive before Christ.

Also, while we are in the park, I think it appropriate to mention how thankful we should be to our National Park Service. Just notice the way in which they have carefully, but unobtrusively, marked out the paths and sights of interest, and have included a special Miwok Braille Trail for the blind.

If you are interested in hiking, this area of Marin County offers a wealth of well-marked trails. Along them in the spring you will discover a wildflower wonderland—Douglas iris, trillium, monkey flowers, blue-eyed grass, Indian paint brush, lupine, and literally dozens of others, including, of course, the California poppy.

And often as you hike along a Mount Tamalpais trail, you will look up from examining a crimson Indian warrior, to gaze at the dramatic skyline of San Francisco far off in the distance. So if you are a hiker or even just a good walker, you should plan to experience the trails of Mount Tamalpais some time during your stay. Trail maps are available right here in the gift shop at Muir Woods.

4:00 p.m. If you came by car, you can experience the park as long as you wish, at least until sunset which is the closing hour. However, for those of you who came either by cab or bus, it is now time to leave. By automobile, simply exit from the park following the well-marked signs back to San Francisco.

Or your Sausalito taxi will take you back to the town square. Here, you should check the ferry schedule posted at the ferry dock on the Bay side of the town square (or telephone 332-6600) for the next departure to San Francisco.

If during the day, you have envied those who were able to travel by car, you should feel much better making your way back by ferry. For while they are driving the 17 freeway miles back to San Francisco, you can relax on the upper deck of the ship, a drink in one hand (cocktails are *de rigueur* on the Bay for many ferry commuters), tossing potato chip crumbs to the hovering gulls with the other. And the Bay at this time of day can be fantastic! For those of you who cannot make the ferry trip today, I have scheduled a Bay cruise for later in your week. No matter how you manage it, a trip on San Francisco Bay should not be missed.

On docking at the San Francisco side, at the old, historic Ferry Building, you might wish to walk across the Embarcadero and drop into the Hyatt Regency Hotel. If you have never seen one of these incredible multi-storied Hyatt lobbies, this is an awesome example—complete with fountains, huge sculptures, and elevators of Buck Rogers design. You might wish another cocktail in the revolving Equinox Room (open from 11 a.m. to 1:30 a.m.) at the top.

6:00 p.m.   I am certain a couple hours of rest after your long day would be welcome right now. Back in your hotel, you can catch the evening TV news and find out what the world has been doing, or write those postcards—it's now or never!

However, if you take a later ferry back from Sausalito or are ready for an early dinner, I have a recommendation within an easy walk of the Ferry Building.

Tadich Grill, 240 California Street (391-2373; open weekdays from 11 a.m. to 9 p.m.; Saturday from 11:30 a.m.), is San Francisco's oldest, most popular, and most famous fish house. It is not, however, our best.

Whenever I talk to a group of visitors, by far the most common questions I am asked refer to seafood: Where is the best place to eat on Fisherman's Wharf? What's the best seafood restaurant in town?

And it's understandable. After all, San Francisco is surrounded by sea and bay. Therefore, you would think that seafood restaurants would be great and plentiful. Plentiful, yes. Great? Well, a few. Tomorrow night, I will take you to my favorite—the Hayes Street Grill.

Of course, great fish can be had in some of our top restaurants, such as Fleur de Lys and Postrio, as well as in some Chinese restaurants specializing in fish.

As for the fish restaurants on the Wharf, I always make an effort when revising this book to try a few to see if they have improved. But after two or three nights of massive plates of decent fish, crowding some of the worst pasta in creation, all awash in the liquid of primarily frozen vegetables, I give up.

And for a few years, I gave up on Tadich, too. They did not appear in the last edition of this guide. But on recent visits, I found the quality had apparently recovered from the slippage of several years ago. Either that or I enjoy the atmosphere so much—as do visitors and natives alike—and I order so carefully, that Tadich is back in my good graces.

Tadich's ancestry dates back to 1849—and they still preserve in a natural way some of that '49er atmosphere. The waiters scurry about in floor-length aprons, the menu is printed daily, the cloth-covered tables contain nothing unessential, the crowds are animated.

In fact, if you arrive much after six, you will find yourself waiting at the tiny, standing-room-only bar, where the crush of imbibing patrons usually develops an infectious camaraderie. Visitors who have not set foot in Tadich in years always recall this "fun" spirit.

At your table, I suggest you strenuously avoid any temptation to stray from plain, simply-done fresh fish. But start off with a dinner salad—a creamy Italian dressing over respectable greens, all topped with tiny bay shrimp. Or the bay shrimp cocktail with a very mild-mannered—too much so for my taste—cocktail sauce.

One thing you can be certain of at Tadich—the fresh fish is *fresh*. So your preference will guide you. I personally favor the charbroiled petrale sole—a local variety of flat fish—moist, with the under skin helping to hold the tender flesh together. During the summer, salmon is certainly the fish of the season. I always request that larger fish, like sea bass—durable enough to take the slight searing of hot coals—be charbroiled. The fragile little sanddabs—about seven to nine inches in length—require the gentler ministrations of sauteeing to preserve their delicacy.

Vegetables are fairly vapid—either from being frozen or just nonchalantly handled. And the tartar sauce—which one famed New York food critic lauded as outstanding—I find hopelessly bland, and overthickened with riced potatoes! However, the potatoes which accompany most fish dishes can be great—not matchstick thin but thick-cut fish fries, nice and mealy in the middle.

The once classic rice pudding has degenerated into a firm rice base topped high with a barely sweetened custard. Try fresh melon in season.

But even with its apparent faults, everyone goes to Tadich. And you should too.

8:00 p.m.   If you did not opt for an early dinner at Tadich, let's consider a couple of other options.

Khan Toke, 5937 Geary Blvd. near 24th Ave. (668-6654; open daily for dinner only; reservations advised), gives you a quick trip to fabled Thailand to experience not only its lovely cuisine but also its gracious manner of dining.

On entering, you remove your shoes—wear loafers for ease—and are then shown to your table, a low lacquered affair with a glass top covering a wealth of Thai wood carvings beneath. These tables have been placed over wells, so that you need not sit cross-legged but upright on soft cushions with your legs in the well. It's extremely comfortable, but getting up can be a little awkward.

The rooms are extremely handsome—panelled in wood, often interspersed with colorful Thai fabrics. Thai artifacts adorn the walls, while a charming garden is in view in the rear. The uniformed waiters work cooperatively in serving you the delicate—at times gentle, at times fiery—cuisine.

Two popular beginnings to any Thai meal are well executed here: tod mun, the classic Thai fried-fish cakes accompanied by a peanut-speckled cucumber condiment, and tom yam goong, a spicy lemon-grass shrimp soup with mushrooms and tomatoes. You may specify the degree of spiciness you wish in the latter. And unless you really know Thai food and love perspiration-creating zest, I would advise caution.

No caution is necessary with the following main courses. I recommend ordering Chinese-style, and having everyone at the table share the various dishes. Such as the sensational gai yang, marinated barbecued chicken with a honey of a honey sauce.

To sample Thai curry, the mus-a-mun is a must: large cubes of beef and sweet potato in a deeply dark coconut milk-red curry, capable of converting even die-hard curry haters. A very mild-mannered dish is the Bangkok prawns in which the shellfish have been marinated in green peppercorns, garlic and cilantro and served over shredded lettuce.

The fried banana, partnered by coconut ice cream dotted with cashew nuts, is as good as this dish can get. Thai beer provides the perfect foil to dampen some of the spiciness you will encounter on this fascinating visit to Bangkok by the Bay. And a moderate check makes this all the more pleasant an evening out. (To reach Khan Toke, simply drive out Geary St.—or take a #38 bus—right to its door.)

Alfred's, 886 Broadway off Mason (781-7058; open nightly for dinner; reservations suggested), has been a favorite San Francisco steak house since 1928. I remember taking my very first dinner date there. She was impressed and ate like a starving Siberian wolf!

Actually, even up through World War II days it was considered primarily an Italian restaurant which featured steaks. But today, although the menu still pays homage to Alfred's Italian origins, it's the superb steaks that keep San Franciscans coming back, and back again.

When you enter Alfred's, it's a little like entering a restaurant time capsule. The walls are plush red—none of the current salmon-grey combo—and chandeliers sparkle overhead. Adjacent to the dining area is a long old-fashioned burnished wood bar, where mighty fine martinis are created.

The menu is a plain-paper job, with an anatomical map of a steer, showing just where your choice of beef originates. But before we get to that auspicious main event, let's look at the preliminaries.

Years ago there must have been hundreds of Italian restaurants in North Beach serving complete dinners at comfortable prices. And almost all of them began with copious antipasto courses. Alfred's still shelters this endangered species of opener.

I had to sample one if for no other reason than sheer nostalgia. And there was calamari vinaigrette, pickled pigs feet, dry salami, mild coppa, mortadella, garbanzo and kidney bean salad, marinated artichokes, stuffed grape leaves, green and black olives, pepperoncini, carrots, celery hearts and radishes! Whew! But the pleasant surprise was the freshness of this gargantuan spread. One of the reasons for the near extinction of this dining dinosaur was that restaurants began to present sadly stale plates—a meaningless, faceless mess. But except for the lame stuffed grape leaves, Alfred's does the old tradition proud.

If you find such a massive opener intimidating—actually it is surprisingly refreshing—then Alfred's classic Caesar salad is certainly the way to go. At Alfred's a trained maitre d' tosses the salad tableside, calling upon just the right quantities of egg, grated cheese, garlicked olive oil, regular olive oil, Worchestershire sauce, anchovies, salt and pepper to dress the perfectly chilled romaine.

A rock shrimp cocktail is another fine starter, but I found the fried zucchini sticks and onion rings combo to be not especially interesting.

But beef is what we came here for, so let your personal taste be your guide to the cut you order. However, there is an "Alfred's Steak," which is a bone-in strip steak. Sort of betwixt a New York strip and a T-bone. It's sensational, even though filet mignon lovers, like me, can seldom be swayed. All Alfred's steaks are graded USDA Choice and cut from corn-fed beef. Aged in Alfred's own coolers, they are broiled over genuine mesquite charcoal for that requisite slightly charred crust. A caveat on the menu warns "Not responsible for steaks ordered cooked more than medium." Amen.

Another Alfred's attribute which endears diners are unusually fine fresh vegetables. When a dieting dining-companion asked if they could serve simply plain steamed vegetables, Alfred's kitchen responded handsomely without hesitation. And a final plus is a wine list far above that encountered in most steakeries. But then, Alfred's has been pleasing beef-eaters for six decades—even through times when blood-rare beef was sneered upon. They must be doing something right.

To get to this very San Francisco restaurant you can travel on a uniquely San Francisco mode of transportation—the cable car. If you are in the Union Square area, simply hop a "Powell Line" cable car and ride it to Broadway. Alfred's is only a few yards down hill.

10:00 p.m. A very popular form of entertainment in San Francisco is its comedy clubs. Here fledgling comedians try out their routines, hopeful that someday they can perform the polished version for Johnny Carson's viewers. And often, comedy greats like Robin Williams—who lives in town—have been known to drop by unexpectedly to test some of their new acts.

Again, the best place to get a current reading on who is appearing where around town and in the entire Bay Area is in the Date Book Section of the Sunday *San Francisco Examiner & Chronicle*. There you will find listings of all jazz joints, nightclubs, and music events as well.

Your Fourth Perfect Day Schedule

9:30 a.m. A Spartan juice-and-coffee breakfast is what's recommended this morning before we embark on our tour through. . .

10:00 a.m. Chinatown! The largest in the Western world. I will personally conduct you on a walking tour of Chinatown and offer three luncheon options.

2:00 p.m. Rest your feet while you give your eyes and ears a treat at either a performance of the symphony, opera, ballet, theater or even a good movie.

5:00 p.m. Wile away the cocktail hour in a downtown aerie from which you can watch the commuter traffic struggle home.

8:30 p.m. Dine at the city's finest California-style grill, indulge in superb French country cooking, or be amused and amazed by exciting "New World" culinary creations served up in a colorful former auto shop.

11:00 p.m. Sprawl in front of your hotel TV to see what has happened in the world since you've been away from it. Then stay tuned for reruns of San Francisco-based shows—by now, you should know your way around better than the movie cameras! But rest up. Tomorrow brings Japantown, Pacific Heights and Union Street.

The Fourth Day of Your
One Perfect Week in San Francisco

9:30 a.m.   If you followed my night-club going recommendation last night, you should appreciate this slightly
delayed opening of your Fourth Perfect Day. Try to forgo
breakfast or at least limit it to a Spartan juice-and-coffee
because we have a wide choice of unusual Chinese
lunches. And to make matters more filling, your choices
for dinner are three of the most exciting restaurants in
town.

10:00 a.m.   Because I will personally conduct you
through San Francisco's world-famous Chinatown, it is
best we begin at that quarter's official entrance—the ornate Chinese gate on the corner of Bush and Grant.

If you are staying either on Nob Hill or in the Union
Square area, it is only a short walk. In fact, the reason our
Chinatown is so popular is that it is centrally located, immediately adjacent to the downtown hub of the city. This,
for example, is not the case in New York City where you
must undertake a lengthy subway or cab ride far from mid-
town Manhattan.

So now it's off to Chinatown. Oh, yes, bring along those
postcards you wrote yesterday. We will pass a post office
where you can mail them so they arrive home before you
do.

As we pass through the dragon-crested Chinatown gate,
a gift from the Republic of China in 1969, try not to notice
the un-Oriental hamburgery and chocolate chippery that
greet you at the entrance. Instead, you might wish to hum
the melody from *Flower Drum Song*—*"Grant Avenue, San
Francisco, California, U.S.A"*—for that is indeed the street
on which we will be concentrating this morning.

With every new edition of this guide, I find that I must

delete yet another ancient shop or two along our Grant Avenue route. The reason is simple: Chinatown is prime real estate and often, after the sale of a building, long-time shop owners find their rents increased astronomically. Thus, the former quaint little bead shop or mom-and-pop grocery is now a bank, jewelry store or McDonald's. Nevertheless, there is still excitement and color to Chinatown that should not be missed.

And while window-shopping is what most visitors do in Chinatown, now and then look up at the wealth of architectural detail—balconies with lace-like grills and a variety of tiled roofs and eaves. For example, number 747 Grant and the large building on the corner of Clay.

Old St. Mary's Church, on the corner of Grant and California, dates from 1854. The original shell of brick, most of which was quarried in China and shipped in sailing vessels across the vast Pacific, withstood the quake which triggered the '06 fire, but the interior was totally gutted. Today, this charming church holds a special place in the affections of all San Franciscans.

Opposite the church on California Street is St. Mary's Square, a sunning spot for financial-district lunchers, watched over by Benny Bufano's imposing statue of Sun Yat Sen.

Further down Sacramento Street at 755, you will find an unusual building housing the Nam Kue Elementary School. Now, back up to Grant Avenue and continue for one block to Clay Street.

Here a short climb up Clay Street for one block takes us to Stockton Street. On the opposite corner you will see a U.S. Post Office from which you can mail those postcards. But more important, immediately next door, at 855 Stockton Street, you will uncover the entrance to the Taoist Kong Chow Temple (take the elevator at the rear of the lobby to the fourth floor).

This is an active temple where you will find worshipers burning incense and sweet oils as offerings to Kwan Ti. For a dollar, you can have your fortune told—it is invariably a rosy one.

Prior to the 1948 election, on visiting the temple Mrs. Harry S Truman was given a good fortune, assuring her that her husband would win. And much to the surprise of everyone, he did! According to the notice at the temple, after she returned to Washington, D.C., she requested a copy of that fortune.

But fortunes aside, the temple with its ornately carved altar is fascinating, and so is the cityscape from its terrace. After enjoying the temple, return back down Clay Street for a half block to Waverly Place and then turn left.

This block of Waverly is one of my favorites. It has avoided the gross commercialism of Grant Avenue. Lined with colorful iron-balconied buildings, it houses many temples and meeting rooms of the various benevolent societies. If you see wisps of smoke rising from upper stories, don't panic—it is just the smoke from incense burning in huge braziers on the balconies. And as you pass the Hop Sing Tong Building, you might hear the sounds of Sinocast, the Chinese-language radio station which broadcasts from here.

At the corner of Waverly Place and Washington Street turn left, and take peek into The Superior Trading Company, 839 Washington. This is a "modern" version of the famed old medicine and herb shops that used to abound on Grant Avenue. I say "modern" because the countless drawers with their mysterious treasures of roots, herbs and spices are conveniently labeled to help the clerk. In ancient herb shops, the owners prided themselves on knowing the contents of each drawer and would have died of shame rather than label them.

At 863 Washington is the Tong Hing Pastry Shop. Its claim to fame—apple pie! Apple pie, that all-American dessert, is a great favorite among the Chinese community, exceeded perhaps only by coconut-custard pies and sponge cakes covered with whipped cream. Chances are you will see all three in this popular shop.

Continuing further up Washington Street, you will return again to Stockton Street, where you turn right. Many years ago, Stockton Street was technically outside the strict confines of Chinatown proper. As the non-tourist-oriented shops were pushed from Grant Avenue by the more lucrative jewelry shops, etc., they regrouped here.

So especially on the far side of Stockton, even though the architecture hardly reflects any Chinese influence, you will suddenly be transported to the Orient. Here are all the food stores with their stacks of greens and oranges spilling onto the sidewalks. There are fish stalls, their smell of the sea commingling with the aroma from cooked-food shops, with their roasted ducks hanging in the windows. Just throw yourself into the throngs of Chinese shoppers as they stock up on fresh produce, fish and poultry.

With the reliance of Chinese cooking on the ultimate in fresh ingredients, daily shopping is a necessity. And the examination some of these women put each vegetable or wall-eyed fish through is remarkable to behold.

A couple of blocks along Stockton brings you to Pacific. If you have not already lunched at Tung Fong, this is a great opportunity. It's only a half block up the street. And a dim sum lunch should not be missed. (For ordering suggestions, see the First Perfect Day.)

Another block further along Stockton, you will find Yuet Lee on the corner of Broadway. This was the late-night Chinese fish restaurant I recommended earlier. If you would like to try it now, again you will find ordering recommendations at the end of the First Perfect Day.

However, my third lunch suggestion is new. And what makes it most interesting is that it offers many dishes in a style of Chinese cuisine seldom encountered elsewhere in the U.S.

Mon Kiang, 683 Broadway (421-2015; lunch and dinner served daily), specializes in the cooking of a people, rather than a province of China.

Centuries ago the Hakka were forced from their Northern China homes, setting up colonies in South China. And like the Louisiana Cajuns, who were transported south from Canada's Acadia, the Hakka retained many of their original ethnic dishes from their ancestral home. And this is what will delight you at Mon Kiang.

For a starter, you should try their beef balls in spinach soup. The beef balls are dense yet somewhat spongy and are served in a clear stock filled with brilliantly green, barely cooked spinach. The contrast between the slightly spicy meat balls and the spinach is marvelous. Fish balls, similar to spoon-sized *quenelles*, are also served in the same manner.

My favorite Hakka dish is the salted baked chicken. This plump fowl is in no way crisp-skinned, as you might imagine a baked bird would be. But rather the skin is soft, as though poached like a classic French *poulet vapeur*. And the meat is gloriously full-flavored. If you complain that today's chickens lack the flavor of those of yesteryear, just try this one. And dip pieces into one of the two sauces provided—the pale one (my favorite) is finely minced garlic and ginger in oil, the other a fiery chili sauce.

Then go on to the wine-flavored beef or chicken—the tender strips of meat are tossed with pickled mustard greens in a piquant, uniquely flavored wine sauce. The outcome is unlike any Chinese dish I have ever experienced. And when I try to quiz a waiter as to its full composition, I get as far as wine and vinegar and then "lots of other things" rings down the curtain on my exploration.

This is more than ample for two, but if you are taking your Chinatown tour in a larger group, you might try some seafood dishes, such as their mixed seafood platter. And if it's crab season, you cannot miss in a Chinese restaurant, whether the chef be Hakka, Cantonese, Hunanese, or Szechwan.

With this Hakka feast, I enjoy Tsing Tao, the mainland China beer. Ambience is zilch—paper napkins, and mostly large tables (which you may have to share). Prices are less than moderate. But the cooking is intriguing and offers you a rare opportunity to relish dishes you will be hard pressed to find elsewhere in America.

Now then, back onto Broadway to continue our tour. But first, let me tell you a little about this famed San Francisco street.

Broadway has always been one of the city's most colorful streets. Many years ago, it was the unofficial boundary between Chinatown and predominately Italian North Beach. And on it, especially a block or so to your right, were superb late-hour dining spots, like New Joe's. The finest minestrone anywhere was ladled out at Dante's Pool Hall. Pinza and other opera greats of the '30s and '40s ate lustily at the old Fior d'Italia, while you went to the Buon Gusto for salted cod and ceci.

And for years it was the heart of the city's nightlife. Famed Finocchio's, the female impersonator show your grandparents probably saw fifty years ago, is still just a few blocks down the street. Off Broadway a couple of blocks was the original Hungry i, not the "erotic sex acts" shop you may spot in a few minutes. In the cellar of the old Hungry i, I was overwhelmed by an unknown New York girl with an extraordinary voice—Barbra Streisand. Mort Sahl as well as Mike Nichols and Elaine May were regulars. And in another nearby basement, an unknown housewife named Phyllis Diller first told of her trials and tribulations in stuffing a turkey. It was quite an era.

Then in the early '60s Broadway made a national splash—Carol Doda went topless at the Condor on the corner of Broadway and Columbus. That seems so tame today, but it ended one era of Broadway and ushered in another.

To compete, other nightclubs began with topless, then bottomless and on down to live sex acts. And the street went downhill fast! The good restaurants (fabulous New Joe's) lost their regular customers, who no longer wanted to come to what had become—in the words of an earlier edition of this guide—"mammary lane." So they closed, giving way to more sleazy clubs, finally attracting more violence and drugs.

Today, you will find many of the old places boarded up and Broadway, especially a block or so nearer the Bay, once queen of San Francisco nightlife, has become a forelorn bag lady. I just hope this phase in the life of Broadway will be short-lived.

Anyhow, right now you need only walk a half block further along Broadway, and turn right to find yourself back on Grant Avenue, Chinatown.

As you head back along Grant Avenue, you might watch for these shops and spots of special interest:

At 1016, The Ginn Wall Company is a hardware store that also carries a goodly amount of Chinese cooking utensils—woks, steamers, etc. At 903 Grant is Fat Ming Company, a stationery shop with a marvelous array of greeting cards from Hong Kong. Decorated with traditional Chinese artwork and characters, but with English messages, they make novel and beautiful greetings. You will also note that just about all the cards feature red extensively. Red is the "good luck" color. Thus, brides too wear red, not white, which is the color for mourning.

At the next street corner, Washington, walk downhill a few yards to number 743 to take a look at the marvelous pagoda-style building, the oldest of its kind in Chinatown. Today it houses the Bank of Canton, but for many years it was the special telephone exchange for Chinatown.

From in front of number 733, there is a wonderful view, capturing San Francisco's past and present. For by looking down Commercial Street, you can see the Ferry Building's old tower situated perfectly in the narrow slit formed by the sheer towers of the Golden Gateway.

Our last Chinatown stop is at 717 Grant, the Chinatown Kite Shop, with kites in the shape of dragons, butterflies, etc., suspended from the ceiling. But little by little the shop's identity is being buried under mounds of tourist paraphernalia, such as T-shirts emblazoned with "My Mom and Dad went to San Francisco and all I got was this dumb T-shirt!" And that is what has happened to Grant Avenue.

2:00 p.m.   After a morning on your feet, I have planned a "sit-down" afternoon. And that means either a play, musical, symphony, opera, ballet or movie—all depending on your preference, the day of the week, as well as what time of year.

If today is almost any Thursday from mid-September to

early June, you might wish to attend an afternoon performance of the famed San Francisco Symphony at Davies Hall in the Civic Center.

Many years ago, the matinee audience consisted predominantly of women who made these performances a social habit. Their custom of wearing "correct" gloves once prompted Papa Pierre Monteux, our legendary former symphony conductor, to remark that he could hardly hear the ladies' applause!

The Thursday afternoon concerts often sell out, so you should plan ahead and purchase your seats either at the City Box Office in the Sherman Clay Music Store (392-4400; small service charge) or directly from the Symphony Box Office in the Davies Hall lobby (431-5400; orders can be charged to major credit cards). Symphony tickets can also often be purchased from the various ticket agencies located in many hotel lobbies.

Davies Symphony Hall is not one of my favorite concert halls. I find the exterior has the appearance of a gigantic bus terminal. Inside things do not improve much. The architects appear to have had curious ideas about traffic flow, designing the enormous sweeping staircase to empty right into a bottleneck. Inside the auditorium proper, acoustics are variable. And it is a pity, since the Symphony under conductor Herbert Blomstedt is sounding better than it has in years.

If your musical interests include the lyric world of grand opera, you must already know you are in a world-class city when it comes to that form of theater.

In the United States, the San Francisco Opera Company is second only to the Metropolitan Opera in quantity of performances and second to none in quality. It has been the American debut company for such legendary superstars as del Monaco, Tebaldi, Rysanek and many others, and its repertory is far more adventuresome than that at the staid Met.

While as of the moment it performs primarily in the fall, from early September to mid-December, General Director Lotfi Mansouri is now advocating breaking up the concentration of fall performances into a longer season to stretch into winter.

As of this writing, there are also plans on the boards to revive the Summer Festival season, which had been in operation a few years ago.

However be warned, tickets for the opera are often extremely hard to come by at the last minute. So if you are reading these pages far in advance of your visit, I suggest you call their box office (864-3330) to see if there will be any performances during your stay.

Whatever tickets are available can be obtained at the opera box office in the Opera House lobby. If they are sold out, you might try one of the independent ticket agencies. Failing this, you can try to unearth a turn-in at the last minute. The Opera performs matinees on Sunday, with an occasional Saturday afternoon performance.

Once inside, the Opera House itself is something to see. While it does not possess the elaborate red damask aura of old-fashioned European houses, it is happily not the cold, unfinished concrete and exposed steel of its contemporary sisters. It has spaciousness, comfort, and fine acoustics (except for the rear of the orchestra, under the balcony overhang). Also, unlike many older theaters, the sight lines are excellent, with only a small section of orchestra and box seats on the extreme sides not having a total view of the stage.

San Francisco is also the home of the nation's longest-running ballet company—the prestigious San Francisco Ballet. Founded in 1933, right after the Opera House was built, it is in residence from the end of January until the beginning of May, with matinees on many Saturdays and Sundays. It also delights children of all ages and knowledgeable balletomanes with performances of *The Nutcracker* throughout December. Under the guidance of Artistic Director Helgi Tomasson, the company has garnered international acclaim and his magical *Sleeping Beauty* had even hardened *New York Times* critics raving.

For information on ballet performances, call 621-3838. Tickets may be purchased through BASS, call 861-5600, or in person at the ballet box office in the Opera House lobby.

As I mentioned on our First Perfect Day outing, the Opera House is a twin structure to the Veterans' Building, across the carriage entrance and garden. Both it and the Opera House served as the site of the signing of the United Nations Charter in April 1945.

While on its upper floors, the Veterans' Building houses the San Francisco Museum of Modern Art, on its main floor is the lovely 1000-seat Herbst Theater. And it is the scene of many concerts, most sponsored by San Francisco Performances. For information on their attractions—from Ameling to Watts—call 398-6449.

The San Francisco musical comedy scene underwent a major restructuring in the late 1970's when Carole J. Shorenstein burst upon the city. Ms. Shorenstein, whose father just happens to own a great deal of downtown San Francisco, including some of the city's largest theaters, launched the "Best of Broadway" series in association with James M. Nederlander. And the city was alive with the sound of music emanating from their three theaters.

However, as the one-time plethora of smash-hit Broadway musicals dwindled down to a precious few—with the notable exception of those by Andrew Lloyd Webber—the "Best of Broadway" began to suffer from a lack of product.

Therefore, at this moment there is no guarantee that there will be a musical playing at either the Curran, Orpheum, or Golden Gate Theater. But check the theater section of the Sunday *Examiner & Chronicle*.

San Francisco has always had a strong theatrical tradition dating back to the '49er days. In fact, the thundering of the miners' heavy boots on the bare wooden floors literally could "bring down the house"!

Post-World War II days found touring companies and a host of small repertory companies (the most famous being the Actor's Workshop) filling the playbills. Today, the old-time Broadway touring companies which once were the domain of Katherine Cornell, Eva Le Gallienne, Tallulah, and others have all but disappeared.

But San Francisco's theater tradition has been kept alive mainly by the American Conservatory Theater and a bevy of "little theaters".

ACT, as it is known, has since its inception operated the historic Geary Theater, a few blocks off Union Square. However, in the '89 Quake, the old theater was badly damaged. And as of this writing, there is still no accurate timetable as to when its marquee will again be lit.

However, this has not daunted the ACT which continues on various other stages around town with its wide-ranging repertory of classics, revivals, contemporary and avant-garde offerings. Many are presented in a highly original and, at times, controversial style. The dominance of local legitimate theater by ACT has also put them in the position of sponsoring what few touring companies there are, which has included England's Old Vic.

For information on ACT presentations and ticket availability, call 749-2ACT.

The list of San Francisco "little theaters" is a long one and includes some extremely fine companies—the Eureka and the Magic, to name just two—which often focus on contemporary concerns and on showcasing the works of new authors. Again, check the "Pink Section" of the Sunday newspaper for performances.

Many people think that going to a movie is a waste of time while on vacation or on a visit to a new city. I disagree. I think that any full week of strictly sightseeing can become tiring if one doesn't stop once in a while to relax and refuel. And for me, there is no better place to lose myself than in a darkened movie house where I can become totally occupied by the images on the screen. And if you find a film you have not seen, you might also discover that viewing it at a matinee is not only a pleasant change of pace but a bargain as well, since many cinemas offer reduced prices for their earliest matinee showings.

If there are no theatrical offerings to interest you this afternoon, you could take a very leisurely stroll through one of our museums, again not trying to see everything in all the galleries but just settling down in front of a few favorites in peace and quiet.

5:00 p.m.   Having spent your afternoon in a darkened theater, a refreshing contrast might be cocktails from a different vantage point.

For this, I recommend the newest alcohol aerie perched atop the Marriott Hotel, on Fourth street right off Market Street. From a cocktail lounge in its juke box-like dome, there are splendid views. And the unusual construction of the windows lend the room an outer-space aura, as though you are in the waiting room of a 21st century rocketport with boarding for the 5:10 to Jupiter about to be announced.

O.K. So what's cooking for dinner?

Well, for this evening I have decided to concentrate on restaurants adjacent to the Civic Center, because that is where the Opera House, Davies Hall, the Herbst Theater and the Civic Auditorium are all located.

Therefore, if you have attended a matinee in any of these theaters, you might wish to have an early dinner in a nearby restaurant. Or if you are attending an evening performance, you may wish to dine in the area and walk to the theater.

And let me assure you, today the convenience of dining near the Civic Center does in no way hamper our selection. Yet, that was totally untrue even ten years ago.

At that time, the Civic Center was a culinary wasteland, with a nearby Doggie Diner often hosting black-tied and bejewelled opera goers. But in recent years, since the completion of Davies Hall, the scene has changed enormously. So much so that the area now boasts some of the city's finest and most popular restaurants.

In fact, their popularity is so great that if you wish to dine in the area before a performance, you must make reservations as far in advance as possible and hope for the best. If you are not attending a performance, reservations are easier to gain after 8:30 when the diners are tucked into

their Davies Hall or Opera House seats. So here they are—
three superb restaurants, totally unalike.

Hayes Street Grill, 320 Hayes Street (863-5545; dinner
served Mondays through Saturdays; lunch served Monday
through Friday; reservations for dinner essential usually a
week in advance). Several years ago "grills" sprouted up in
San Francisco like mushrooms after a spring rain. What
fed this incredible invasion was primarily a change in eat-
ing habits—down with blood-red slabs of beef and thick-
sauced dishes and up with fresh fish and chicken done
over mesquite.

The Hayes Street Grill rode into town on this band-
wagon and has been its unchallenged leader ever since.
And to my way of thinking, which is shared by thousands
of San Franciscans, it is the finest fish restaurant in the
city.

The decor is classic California grill—lean and clean.
And the service is cast in the same mold. There is a small
basic menu, but the blackboard's daily specials are what
most diners follow. For example, it can offer a mind-
boggling black bean soup or a salad of red and yellow
beets tossed in walnut oil.

Salads, by the way, are never less than sensational here,
consisting of the finest greens available anywhere. Also,
mussels or clams steamed in a variety of ways are delicious
openers. Or the sweetest of in-the-shell prawns lolling
atop marinated artichoke hearts. Or spicy Creole crab
cakes. Or. . . I could go on and on.

For main courses, the fish is always fresh. If you like
swordfish, this is the place for you—more moistly tender a
fish you could not find. Your choice of two or three sauces
are optional gildings. And, if you have never had shark
(*Jaws* be damned) these beauties are to be loved.

But even though fish occupies the place of honor, do not
pass up the meat dishes, especially if it happens to be their
barbecued baby back ribs, a mammoth portion with each
rib permeated by a luxurious sauce, which might count ap-
ricot preserves amongst its secret ingredients. Or a thick,
juicy veal chop, basking in a rich porcini mushroom sauce.

The Hayes Street is forever receiving "people poll" awards for the best French fries in town. And for once *vox populi* is right!

When it comes to dessert, I shield my eyes from the blackboard's seductive enticements, such as a voluptuous pumpkin custard with praline sauce, and remain faithful to my favorite dessert in town—creme brulee. Just break through that crackling caramel crust and dip into that immoral creamy custard. Indecent! The wine list offers you fine bottlings from some of California's great but lesser known cellars. A truly superb restaurant in a plain brown wrapper.

Zola's, 395 Hayes Street at Gough (864-4824; open nightly except Sunday; reservations a must), is the Hayes Street Grill's major rival for pre-performance diners. And little wonder, it serves what is primarily country-French cuisine with an incomparable elegance of style.

The room itself is big, bright and airy. And if you dine early, sun will still be streaming in the windows. The service is exceptionally attentive and an owner-maitre d' is a font of information on wines.

The menu is rather limited—especially a pre-performance version—but endless in creativity. For example, finger-sized cuts of lamb breast are slightly breaded, sauteed to a glowing brown and served with a vinaigrette enhanced by lots of minced cornichon and capers. Or a soft polenta, molten mascarpone cheese hidden in its interior, is topped with expertly grilled wild mushrooms. A guest once let out such an audible sigh when encountering tiny figs, enwrapped in the finest prosciutto, and slightly broiled, that heads turned! With them were toasts of peppercorn bread (Zola's sensational breads are from the *ne plus ultra* of local bakeries, Berkeley's Acme) topped with gleaming slices of marinated goat cheese.

Although Zola's does not specialize in fish dishes, they produce some of the finest in the city. For example, an imperial king salmon, steamed in white wine, and enthroned upon a ratatouille couch. For a meat main course, blushing pink rectangular lamb slices are becomingly scented with cumin and coriander and simply served with exquisitely sauteed spinach. To add a fillip of fun, a side ramekin holds a cassoulet-like cranberry bean gratin.

For desserts, the risotto souffle cake with nectarine sauce is unforgettable. This most ethereal of cheese cakes resembles a cupcake, crested with real whipped cream (of course!) and moated with a puree of fresh nectarines. But then, I should not single out this one dish as memorable. Zola's can provide one of your most memorable dinners in San Francisco. Not to be missed.

Six Ninety, 690 Van Ness Ave (255-6900; lunch daily except Saturday; dinner nightly from 5:30 to 10:30—9:00 on Sunday; reservations essential), is not the place to dine if blaring music and a hazardous noise level bug you as they do me, especially after a classical music performance.

Yet, 690 is a sensational restaurant—the creation of San Francisco's most famed young-Turk chef (he even does Dewar's Scotch ads!)—Jeremiah Tower. Mr. Tower has just about cornered the market for fine cuisine on this part of Van Ness Avenue.

His flagship, Stars, is right down the street and is certainly his most renowned operation. And while Stars is one of the most popular dining scenes in town, and pleases local food writers, I find its output unpredictable—especially at the price. So Stars does not shine in this Guide. (Although, I do discover more accuracy—and reasonable pricing—on a post-performance supper menu.)

But 690 is more a happening than a restaurant. "Colorful" is a vast understatement. The former auto carburetor shop is alive with tropical colors: huge murals of bikini-clad bodies encircle the high ceiling and there are faux fish and bedazzlingly plumed parrots everywhere with two big, bright red British phone booths (operable) at the ends of the vast bar. The service is efficiently swift and performed by young men and women with hairdos and togs that blend right in with the ambience.

When I first asked a waiter the name of the style of cuisine I was about to indulge in—certainly the menu's offerings were unclear on classification—he responded "New

World". And after dining at 690, I think he may have coined a new culinary term for this amalgam of cooking styles and ingredients—Caribbean, Oriental and even some African—which is fun-loving and exciting. And most important, expertly executed.

So let's start our adventure in "New World" cuisine with fried pearl-sized scallops, accompanied by straw-thin green asparagus. The same asparagus shows up a few nights later, but this time topped by a Thai-accented, spicy quasi-raw beef salad. Superb! The coconut-milk marinated chicken satay is the most moist and toothsome I have ever encountered. The lemon chicken egg rolls give lessons in the fine art of deep-frying most Chinatown chefs should be forced to attend. Then there is a spicy fish fry with Chinese black bean sauce in which the Orient meets Jamaica.

For main courses, one night everyone at my table demands more of my sauteed rock shrimp. The shrimp are lovingly handled—not underdone as some misguided chefs now think proper—and served with superb Basmati rice, flavored with red curry, basil and mint. Totally weird, but delicious, are tiny saffroned new potatoes, incorporated into this exotic concoction. It comes precariously close to "dartboard cooking," but it works!

I do not mind passing off portions from the huge order to one guest, provided I am repaid with meltingly tender slices of a humungusly thick grilled pork chop. (I am finally outgrowing my mother-instilled fear of underdone pork.) Surmounting this Mt. Fuji of pork is an apple-dominated fruit chutney and surrounding it are sauteed bitter greens. Then there's a Maine lobster, hacked into huge pieces—shell and all—sauteed in coconut milk with basil and mint, and served with a zesty, reddish coleslaw.

Desserts are tropically minded with passion fruit pie and a velvety banana cream, the crust of which is lined with chocolate.

690 presents probably the most off-the-wall—sorry, "New World"—cuisine in town, capable of arousing even the most jaded palate. But the surroundings are as big, bright and boisterous as the cooking. So, bring ear plugs if

you must, but here's your chance to experience a unique type of cuisine. Because Mr. Tower has indeed discovered a New World.

11:00 p.m.   Again, it has been a long day—with even more walking planned for tomorrow. So my suggestion now is to head back to your hotel, sprawl out on your bed and perhaps catch the late news on TV—if you really care to know what has been happening in the real world.

And then stay tuned for some of those reruns of shows like "Streets of San Francisco" or any of the dozens of films which have used this most photogenic of all American cities as their backdrop. And since you are such a San Francisco hand by now, try to spot the geographic errors, such as having a police chase begin at the Golden Gate Bridge Plaza and end two seconds later atop Nob Hill. You and I both know that's not quite possible. Right? Pleasant dreams.

Your Fifth Perfect Day Schedule

9:00 a.m. Only a light breakfast, because we will be having an early lunch.

10:00 a.m. A walking tour of Japantown, where yesterday and tomorrow meet in the flutter of cherry blossoms along a peaceful mall, and in the glare and blare of electronics equipment in a modern trade center.

12:00 noon Lunch at an authentic Japanese restaurant where both novice and Nipponphile can savor the finest tempura and gyoza in town.

1:30 p.m. A journey through San Francisco's past, strolling down the tree-shaded streets of famed Pacific Heights, one of the poshest urban neighborhoods in America.

3:30 p.m. Union Street where today's chic shops are housed on a yesterday street. Late afternoon cocktails in one of its famed "watering spots."

6:00 p.m. If you wish to stay in the area for an early dinner, there is a steakery that's strictly San Francisco and an Italian trattoria that's Italianissimo.

8:00 p.m. If you prefer a later dinner, then visit a unique restaurant presided over by one of America's leading authorities on Chinese cuisine. Of if you had an early dinner and are still on the go, how about taking in San Francisco's own, inimitable *Beach Blanket Babylon*?

The Fifth Day of Your
One Perfect Week in San Francisco

9:00 a.m. Today will be your chance to experience more of the feel of this marvelous city—through the soles of your feet! It will be a day that can be savored only by a good deal of walking—ambling down a stone-paved Japanese mall, strolling through the quiet tree-shaded streets of luxurious Pacific Heights, browsing in and out of the crazy-quilt warren of shops along Union Street. In all, today will be a kaleidoscope of sights, uniquely San Francisco.

Of all the itineraries in this book, today's was the most difficult to map out. In leading you from one area to another, I wanted to avoid any strenuous climbs—a near-impossible feat in hilly San Francisco.

But by following my directions, you can effortlessly take the day in stride. There will be no need for a car, for we will travel by foot and public transportation. Be sure you have a good supply of change, because you need the correct fare on the city's buses. The other requisite is a good pair of walking shoes.

10:00 a.m. After a light breakfast, walk to Union Square and, on the corner of Powell and Geary, board a #38 Geary bus (not the limited, but the regular #38).

Ask the driver to call out Webster Street for you. If he remembers, your destination should be reached in about fifteen minutes. On leaving the bus, cross Webster Street (note the street sign is also written in Japanese characters), turn right, and enter the doors of 1581 Webster.

In the 1950's, when Japanese trade with the United States began to burgeon and tourism across the Pacific took on the aspects of a commute run, Japanese business interests drew up plans for a culture-and-trade center that would not only showcase Japanese products, but cement stronger cultural ties with San Francisco.

Discussions, plans and the inevitable delays seemed to go on without end. Finally, the three-block long complex, which you have just entered, materialized.

Whether the idea was too grandiose or the site, appropriately located in San Francisco's "Japantown," was too distant from downtown shopping and foot traffic, the success the planners envisioned has never been achieved.

For example, the enormous Kabuki Theater, which was launched with glittering imported Japanese reviews, bit the dust shortly after opening. It has now been converted into a eight-screen movie complex.

And while the Miyako Hotel, which towers over the east end of the center, enjoys capacity business, the trade center itself does not seem to attract too much interest. I suspect the lack of great success can be attributed also to the center's obvious touristy air, with bazaar-style shops. Nevertheless, the center is well worth a brief walk-through and you can start by climbing the stairs directly in front of you.

On reaching the upper level, proceed to the left across the covered bridge. Directly before you on the east side of the bridge you will find one of my favorite stops in the center, the Ikenobo Ikebana Society Headquarters.

Ikebana is the art of arranging flowers. And here, in the showcase windows, you can feast your eyes on a few outstanding examples. Practitioners of this delicate art form can achieve more grace and beauty with one iris, a single leaf and a bent twig, than I have ever seen anybody do with two dozen long-stem roses!

If you are interested in learning more about the age-old art and traditions of ikebana, here is your opportunity. The society headquarters also stocks many vases especially suited for ikebana arrangements.

However, another feast for the eye, if not for the pocketbook, is the Murata Pearls displayed right across the way. Only a few doors away from the serene, frozen poetry of ikebana, you will come in contact with the jazzy, garish glitter of the dozens of Japanese TV sets currently on the market.

Exit from the west wing of the center onto the Peace Plaza, with the Peace Pagoda rising above its reflecting pool. Here you might wish to sit a moment and look out over the western half of the city. There is little need to bother with the east wing of the center since it only houses less of the same.

Directly across Post Street from the Peace Plaza is the heart of what once was Japantown.

In 1907, when the Japanese colony resettled here in the "Western Addition" after the '06 fire, the buildings had no oriental flair. Unlike Chinatown, which was devastated in the fire and rebuilt with nods to Chinese architectural styles, Japantown consisted of Victorian wood houses dating from the late 19th century.

The fire never reached here. By dynamiting Van Ness Avenue, it was confined to what we know as the downtown area and Nob Hill. When these old wood buildings began to deteriorate beyond repair, nondescript, more modern dwellings and shops replaced them.

Then, several years ago, instead of waiting for the old structures on this block of Buchanan Street to tumble one by one, they were razed and a Japanese village street rose in their place. Down the center of the wide mall curves a serpentine pattern of stones, connecting two fountains made of stone and iron. The cherry blossom trees and azaleas bloom in the spring and if you are here at that time of year, you can watch their blossoms flutter earthward as you sit on one of the benches.

The shops bordering the mall sell today's Japanese electronic products and the like, but they also contain some fine examples of folk art and kimonos. It's a pleasant place to enjoy a sunny San Francisco day.

Before you take in the mall, however, cross Post Street and turn right along the street's north side. There are a couple of shops you might enjoy browsing through.

For example, on the corner is Soko Hardware. Here you will find not only the usual hardware items but also all manner of supplies, pots and planters for bonsai growers.

Further down the street at number 1656 Post is the Uoki Sakai Company. In this grocery store, you can view the finest and freshest of vegetables. And if you think you have sampled just about every known product of our earth, just glance through the displays of gobo, daikon, hakusai and other roots and greens, all part of Japanese gardening and cuisine.

Now, retrace your steps to the mall. As you amble up the slight incline, you may wish to check the dates on the posters announcing festivals in the community. If one is happening during your stay, a return visit might be in order to witness some time-honored traditions.

For example, during the last week of April, Japantown bursts into cherry-blossom festivities with the Sakuramatsuri Festival. Colorfully garbed in kimonos and other classic Japanese costumes, the participants parade before a backdrop of stately Victorian houses—another uniquely San Francisco happening.

You will also notice that, as in Kyoto and Tokyo, many of the restaurants display in their windows remarkably accurate plastic facsimiles of the dishes they serve. This is so the uninitiated can see precisely what they will be served.

Continue on up the mall to Sanko at 1758 Buchanan Street. Inside you will discover a treasure trove of modern Japanese wares—sake sets, rice bowls, tea pots, etc., which make lovely, yet relatively inexpensive, gifts for friends back home.

The Japan Trading Co., at 1762, is another interesting stop for those interested in authentic Japanese interior decor items, such as shoji screens.

When you reach the top of the mall, cross Sutter Street to the Koyama Super. This Japanese supermarket specializes in a wide variety of tuna, favored for sashimi, as well as octopus and other denizens of the deep. In the far left corner is a tiny sushi counter, where cold rice and seaweed are used as the major ingredients to create a style of snack food, uniquely Japanese.

On leaving the Koyama Super, be sure to take a look at the two buildings almost directly across Sutter Street (Nos. 1771-1777 and 1782-1787).

Both were constructed in the 1880's as "double houses" with each house later turned into a duplex. They are fine examples of Victorian San Francisco architecture.

Now, walk back down the right-hand side of the mall, browsing through some of the shops, such as the Paper Tree at 1743. In this stationery store you will find the papers and instructions necessary for origami, the Japanese art of paper folding, which make for unusual gifts. And further down the mall you might investigate Genji, at number 1731, and the N. B. Kimono Store, at 1715, both specializing in these graceful Japanese robes.

At the bottom of the mall, turn right a few feet and you will find yourself at one of the finest Japanese restaurants in San Francisco—Sanppo, 1702 Post Street (346-3486; lunch and dinner daily except Monday; no credit cards). And since it is open for lunch—which is what you should be considering about now—just walk right in.

12:00 noon.   When you enter Sanppo, you could be entering any one of a thousand small restaurants in Japan. To say the place is clean is slanderous—it is immaculate. The waitresses dart around each other as though performing a ballet choreographed for swallows. And the cooking is superb, especially the tempura which is peerless in town.

To the uninitiated, tempura is but one style of Japanese cooking, one in which a whole range of seafoods and vegetables can be covered with a light batter and then quickly deep-fried. It sounds simple enough. But to insure the correct gossamer lightness and to avoid any signs of greasiness, a chef must have a built-in stopwatch. You will discover Sanppo's excellent tempura for yourself when a plate of shrimp, sweet potato slices and other fresh vegetables, all encased in their light batter-cocoons, is placed before you.

In fact, you might wish to split an order of tempura as a

first course and then proceed to other dishes, such as the gyoza. Almost every ethnic variety of cooking has some manner of meat in pastry—Italy has its ravioli, Russia its pelmeni, China its kuo-tieh, and Japan its gyoza. Gyoza is ground pork touched with garlic, enveloped in a paper-thin dough, and fried on one side only. Delicious!

In salmon season, do not miss the magic a great Japanese chef can perform on this often mishandled fish. And speaking of fish, Sanppo is also an ideal place for those who admire sashimi (raw fish), because if you are fully acquainted with this great delicacy, you will appreciate Sanppo's masterful presentation, a delight to both eye and palate.

Sanppo is an ideal restaurant for both the newcomer to Japanese cuisine as well as the Nipponphile, at moderate prices. (By the way, if Japanese cuisine is not your cup of tea, read ahead. For this evening, I recommend a totally Italian trattoria which you will pass on the next leg of your walking tour—Jackson Fillmore Trattoria. And it's open for lunch Tuesday through Saturday.)

1:00 p.m.   When you leave Sanppo, turn right and walk two blocks to Fillmore Street. As you near Fillmore, it is a good time for me to point out another attraction of the Trade & Cultural Center which is traditionally Japanese, but of which you cannot avail yourself right this moment—a shiatsu massage.

Located in the far west end of the center is Kabuki Hot Spring (922-6000), a Japanese massage center. Here you can bask in the tension-releasing euphoria of a hot tub and sauna, followed by the shiatsu massage. This method concentrates on pressure points in the body rather than on the overall body-caressing usually associated with American or European massages. And you will find no hanky-panky at Kabuki—try the downtown area for that!

At Fillmore Street, turn left one block to the nearest bus stop, on the Geary Street overpass. Board a #22 bus, asking the driver to announce Jackson Street.

Actually, it would be great fun to walk these nine blocks,

but it probably would take its toll on your energies which you will need for later on. So sit back and relax while you observe the incredible cultural mix in the shops and restaurants along the way. For on this section of Fillmore Street no one ethnic group has proprietary rights.

You will see Japanese restaurants (the last outposts of Japantown), soul-food kitchens, Chinese lunch counters, antique-junk dealers, recycled clothes shops, amidst chic boutiques and restaurants on this vibrant revitalized street. However, by the time your bus reaches Jackson Street, the neighborhood suddenly becomes less commercial—for you are on the threshold of Pacific Heights, one of the poshest urban neighborhoods in America.

1:30 p.m.   Leave the bus at Jackson Street. A few doors up the street is the Jackson Fillmore Trattoria, where you might wish to lunch if you passed up Sanppo. I have it scheduled as one of your three choices for dinner this evening, so you should read on for recommendations.

Keep walking up Fillmore to Pacific Avenue. Turn left on Pacific and you find yourself on a tree-shaded street, light-years removed from the atmosphere of only a few short blocks away.

Here, the residential architecture varies greatly in style from the Classical Revival beauties at numbers 2418 and 2420 to the false-fronted Italianate of the Leale House at number 2475. Queen Anne, Baroque, and English are all to be seen.

But more than lessons in architecture, these grand homes represent the wealth and taste of the founding families of San Francisco who built most of them in the closing years of the last century, high on these heights commanding a view of the entrance to the Bay, just as feudal lords built their castles on equally strategic points along the Rhine and Danube. You can share this eagle's-nest view by glancing down Steiner Street to the Bay and the hills beyond.

Five blocks along Pacific, turn right down Broderick Street to Broadway. Yes, this is the same street which houses the roaring, neon-bedecked topless joints of North Beach. But the loudest sounds you may hear in this part of town probably will belong to the electric clocks of the silent Rolls-Royces as they glide by.

Some of the most grandiose houses in San Francisco will be found on the next two blocks, to your left. For example, just look at the one at 2901! One block beyond, Broadway ends at a gate to the Presidio.

So here, turn right and walk down the stairs alongside the Presidio fence to Vallejo, one block below. This is one of my favorite spots in the city. The beautiful landscaping bordering the stairs, ablaze with color in the spring and summer, is a magnificent foreground for the sweeping Bay view before you. Hope you took along that camera.

At Vallejo Street, turn right and continue two blocks to Broderick; then downhill two blocks to Union Street.

3:30 p.m.   At this point, you have a decision to make. If you feel that the pre-lunch walk combined with the one-hour tour through Pacific Heights have proven too much for your stamina, you can simply board a #45 bus and ride back to Union Square downtown.

Or, if you are still game—and I hope you are—you can turn right and proceed along Union Street, up the slight rise and over the top.

Years ago, Union Street was a very sedate shopping area, filled mostly with little antique stores run by quiet-spoken gentlefolk. Then, some "with-it" boutiques began intermingling with the antiques.

In their wake came trendy little restaurants and singles bars, the "watering spots" which cater to the young swingers in search of each other. And Union Street took on a Carnaby Street flair.

But then, as always, the "in-ness" began to become old hat. The South of Market (SOMA) scene began to attract the Yuppie night-life crowd. And Union Street became less hectic.

Today, what you will find is a street somewhat reverting to its past. This six-block stretch still has plenty of interesting chic shops, some watering stops that now appear almost venerable, and some restaurants whose quality has withstood fads, such as Doidge's Kitchen at number 2217, a breakfast favorite.

But if, as I described it in an earlier edition, "the fun and funky, garish and glamorous, sedate and insane" Union Street has changed, I think it is for the best.

Before you proceed to enjoy Union Street, you might wish a calm moment to rest your feet by passing through the lych gate into the courtyard of St. Mary the Virgin's Episcopal Church at the corner of Union and Steiner. In this oasis, the silence is broken only by the splashing of waters from an artesian well into a fountain basin.

Now, on to Union Street. I will not provide you with a door-to-door guide because trendy shops along here have always had unpredictable "shelf lives" and this period of transition will bring even more change.

However, I will introduce you to some outstanding shops on Fillmore Street, right off Union, that have been here for years and will certainly be impervious to any change. So on the corner of Fillmore, take a short side trip downhill.

At 3041 Fillmore you will find Mark Harrington, known for the finest in crystal and all manner of stemware. And further down Fillmore, in the next block at number 3131, is T. Z. Shiota, one of the city's most respected oriental art shops. And as you head back up to Union Street, on the even-numbered side, you come across (at number 3028) Shibata's, another excellent oriental art dealer.

Back up at Union Street, I leave you to browse on your own. But as in Chinatown, don't keep your eyes riveted only on tempting shop windows. Look up at the buildings themselves. While the window displays may be of the latest hair styles or *haute couture* fashions, the buildings, such as number 1981, are charming old relics, many dating from the late 1800's.

Also keep in mind that whenever you tire, you can always catch the #45 bus which takes you back to the Union Square area.

The last thing I want to mention is one of the most unusual houses in San Francisco, the Octagon House. Located right off Union at 2645 Gough (five blocks from Fillmore), this eight-sided structure dates from 1861 and its unusual shape was due to the then popular belief that the octagon represented good luck. It now houses a museum and is owned by the National Society of Colonial Dames.

Naturally, if thirst overcomes you along your Union jaunt, you can easily stop in at one of the numerous "watering holes" such as the popular Perry's at number 1944 and, in the meantime, decide on where you will dine this evening.

6:00 p.m.   I thought that after all the walking, you might enjoy an early dinner this evening. Therefore I have two recommendations—both excellent in their own way and both very San Francisco—located not that far away from where you are right now. If you prefer to return to your hotel, a third recommendation is a couple blocks off Union Square.

Izzy's Steak and Chop House, 3345 Steiner Street (563-0487; open for dinner nightly; reservations), is my favorite casual beefery. It is named after Izzy Gomez, a local saloon-keeper celebrity who ran something of a notorious greasy-spoon, downtown eatery back when—I think in the '20s and '30s. Before my time.

The original Izzy's greasy food was popularized by some sensational goings-on—a stabbing, raids, etc. So I did not quite understand why anyone would resurrect Izzy's name as a come-on for a steakhouse.

But when I first entered the joint, I found that the owners had not only invoked Izzy's name but had re-created an atmosphere that harkens back to Izzy's time.

The first thing that hit me was the fact that I would not want to be in the place during an earthquake. Because rimming the ceiling is a vast display of beer bottles. And on a shoulder high ledge, that runs throughout the dining area, is a continuous parade of employable steak condiments—

hot sauces, pickles, mustards, relishes, etc. (However, iron-
ically Izzy's is located only a block from the heart of the
Marina, which was the area hardest hit in the October '89
quake. And while it was closed for a while because gas
leaks in the neighborhood forced the shutting of their
mains, it sustained literally no physical damage! Those
bottles are still there!)

The place is also filled with old-time San Francisco
memorabilia affixed to walls painted to look time-worn.
Above the bar, a television set is perpetually tuned to some
sports event somewhere. While at the bar, good drinks are
mixed. Make mine a Bombay gin martini, up with one
olive. (I am a traditionalist!)

At your table, the sourdough bread will be thick and
correctly crusty; the menu rather short and simple—steaks
and chops. The smiling service is swift, constantly super-
vised by a manager who seemingly takes no holidays.

Now a confession. Even though I have dined at Izzy's
more times than at perhaps any restaurant in this book,
my knowledge of its menu is not very comprehensive. Because I always order basically the some thing.

I generally start with their a la carte house salad. The
greens are green, the dressing tends to be very mustardy—
maybe they even add some pureed onion—but slices of
raw carrot help calm it. The only other opener I have had is
their prawn cocktail, where the prawns are well handled
and the cocktail sauce ablaze with horseradish. In fact, unless you really enjoy five-alarm cocktail sauces, I would
ask them to omit the extra dollop of horseradish on top.

Unlike pricier a la carte steakhouses, Izzy's offers you
your choice of creamed spinach (quite good; not over-
nutmegged) or roasted carrots and onions (so nice to get
away from those garlicked and oily squash melanges).
Also your choice of potatoes. And while their paper-
wrapped baked potato can be fine, I always opt for their
special potatoes, sort of an O'Brien-au gratin potato dish
that is hearty and flavorful.

As for steaks, I usually take the filet mignon. As in any
steakhouse, each piece of beef can vary in quality. But

when it is at its best, Izzy's is the equal of any in town—buttery soft with true beef flavor. You could not ask for more in a 21-day, dry-aged steak at any price. I have found the New York slightly more variable.

I understand Izzy's also produces fine veal and lamb chops, but the only main course that has caused me to stray from my steaks is the thick-cut, blood-rare roast beef, which is served on weekends only.

For dessert, nothing can seduce me from the creme brulee. Certainly a runner-up to the glorious one I introduced you to at the Hayes Street Grill last night.

Always packed with locals, always noisy, always friendly, always comfortable—Levis or tie, no matter—Izzy's is a great steak joint. (To reach Izzy's from our Union Street walking area, simply head back up Union to the west one block beyond Fillmore Street to Steiner. Turn right on Steiner for about four short blocks. After dinner at Izzy's, you can return to the downtown Union Square area simply by catching a #30 bus on Chestnut Street right around the corner.)

Jackson Fillmore Trattoria, 2506 Fillmore Street (346-5288; lunch served Tuesday through Saturday; dinner nightly except Monday; reservations for three or more at dinner), is a true trattoria. There's a counter, which is on a first-come-first-served basis, and a few booths. There is no decor *per se*, but the energy level more than makes up for it.

Along with your menu, the waiter will plunk onto the table some bruschetta, an appetizer I first encountered in a hole-in-the-wall trattoria on the outskirts of Agrigento, Sicily. And while in some local Italian restaurants you may now order it, here as in Sicily the toasted, garlic-rubbed bread, topped with fresh tomato and doused with olive oil is a freebie. Its rustic simplicity and natural flavors are happy harbingers of what is to come.

The menu is divided into two sections: a handwritten daily section and a printed standard repertory. I try to remain in the daily special portion as much as possible. For there I can be rewarded with some wonderful seasonal specialities. However, I usually cross over to their stuffed artichoke, flattened and packed with minced tomato, and blanketed with garlicky bread crumbs. For a lighter cold appetizer, I favor the poached prawns resting comfortably on a bed of arugula. Or a trattoria standby, crunchy-crusted fried mozzarella enveloped in a dark tomato sauce.

Stellar pastas also appear, such as penne al Siciliano, in which the hearty tubular pasta is treated to a tomato sauce, darkened and enriched by olives and eggplant. On the other hand, I have also been charmed by the most delicate homemade ravioli-like tortelli, filled with ricotta and pieces of fresh asparagus and prosciutto, and topped with melted butter and chopped onion. Totally un-Sicilian and totally beautiful.

But if you happen to hit an evening when they have drunken rice—riso al ubriaco—don't miss it. Precisely cooked in red wine, it is flavored with tiny pieces of spicy red sausage and herbs! Another riso dish I relished one time, was a far more mild-mannered concoction flecked with pieces of fresh crab. *Buonissimo!*

Or if you wish a hot soup, because your day's outing had been through fog-shrouded streets, then something like their minestra rustica—a reviving melange of Tuscan white beans, Swiss chard, tomato and sage—will warm the cockles of your heart.

Again, as with most Italian restaurants both here and abroad, meat dishes can be a letdown. But not the chicken alla Siciliano—tenderly sauteed in white wine with plenty of capers, green olives, garlic, lemon and prosciutto. Or the mahi mahi, in which Hawaii's favorite fish goes to the devil—fra diavolo—and loves it!

For dessert, the tiramisu—chocolate, cheese and cream gone amok—is champion. Also I love their made-to-order zabaglione, but I ask that the fresh fruit they place at the bottom of the glass be omitted. Plenty of wine on hand, and their house selections are usually both priced right and taste right with their cuisine.

No restaurant is ever perfect. Years ago, I sent back a horrendously over-salted first course at France's exalted and three-starred Moulin de Mougins. And sometimes a dish in this funny, wonderful trattoria can go astray. But minor mishaps cannot force Jackson Fillmore from the numero uno spot on my list of San Francisco Italian trattorias. Not to be missed!

To reach Jackson Fillmore from our walking tour of Union Street it is best to take a short bus ride to avoid climbing Fillmore Street, one of the steepest in town. You may board a #22 Fillmore bus at Union and Fillmore that will take you almost to the door of the restaurant. After stuffing yourself, you may return directly to the downtown Union Square area by boarding a #3 Jackson bus on the corner of Jackson and Fillmore and it will take you to within a block of Union Square.

Or if either of the robust dinners at Izzy's or Jackson Fillmore have rejuvenated you—after gallivanting all over Japantown, Pacific Heights and Union Street—you might enjoy taking in a performance of San Francisco's perennial and ever-popular musical revue, *Beach Blanket Babylon* (421-4222; reservations recommended) which plays at the Club Fugazi, 678 Green Street in North Beach. This very funny, uniquely San Francisco company puts on a show full of music and crazy costumes that should be beginning just about now.

For those of you who returned to downtown San Francisco directly from the day-long walking tour, I will not leave you high and dry without a place to dine. No, I will direct you to a another unique San Francisco gustatory experience.

8:00 p.m.   China Moon Cafe, 639 Post Street (775-4789; dim sum lunch and full-menu dinners served Tuesday through Saturday; reservations necessary except for counter seats), has a layout similar to Jackson Fillmore. There is a counter, where seats are open on a first-come basis, and there are booths which must be reserved. Both restaurants are personal favorites of mine because of their superb cuisine. But there all similarities end.

China Moon is the creation of Barbara Tropp, America's

Caucasian maven of Chinese cuisine whose *"The Modern Art of Chinese Cooking"* is a "must have" for cookbook collectors. And unless she is off giving cooking demonstrations, it will be Ms. Tropp who will supervise the dishes that emerge from the kitchen.

Her theory of harmony in Chinese cooking—a culinary yin and yang—is also carried out in the decor of this simple, little restaurant, which has not given up its lunchcounter layout. Colors are muted, some fine Chinese art decorates the walls and a huge paper dragon stretches across the long narrow ceiling.

If there ever was a "personal statement" restaurant, this is it. For on its short menu—minuscule by regular Chinese standards—Ms. Tropp displays a totally distinctive amalgam of oriental and occidental flavors and textures. And when it comes to dessert, she abandons completely those Chinese sweet dishes I for one could never understand and tempts you with mouth-watering Western creations. And there is cappuccino and espresso, too!

But please don't misunderstand. This is not some bastardized Chinese fare. For that, go to one of the chop suey houses in Chinatown. This is serious and gloriously creative Chinese cooking, unlike any you have ever had.

Among the four or five first course choices you may be offered (the menu changes almost weekly) is usually some form of exquisite egg rolls, crispy shells holding a wealth of various ingredients. One night's filling may consist of a vegetable-meat melange, while on another occasion it might be minced chicken, glass noodles and fresh chilies.

A Hunan plate fascinates you with an array of cold, primarily pickled hors d'oeuvres, each with its own inimitable character. There are spicy red onion rings, fire-dried sweetly-coated walnuts and pecans, lemon-pickled daikon rounds and sensational dry-fried szechwan string beans. Another awesome appetizer are the crescent moon turnovers, highly buttery pastry holding within a slightly gingery pork mixture. These delicacies are so fragile, they crumble under the pressure of chopsticks.

There is always a soup selection and it can be a spectacular pinwheel soup—a breathtakingly beautiful stock, filled with mushroom slices and upon which float cross-sections of a forcemeat layered between a celestine-type egg pancake. Fantastic!

For main courses, the succulent pork in strange-flavored sauce has been casserole-cooked until the meat literally falls from the bones. And the "strange flavored sauce" is not strange but lovely—spicy hot with flecks of red pepper, flavored with soy, ginger and garlic. Served with it is possibly the best rice you will ever encounter in a Chinese restaurant—steamed in perhaps a stock to impart an Italian risotto character. The ultimate bok choy—virginal in purity—is the ideal foil for the fiery pork. Another winner is the steamed Thai-marinated fresh prawns, softer in texture than usual, and perfectly set off by a bed of wok-seared onions, leeks, and Napa cabbage. The rice this time has a glorious pine-nut backtaste.

In a sandpot, chicken breast nuggets are wedded to lotus root, fennel, spinach, and glass noodles by a coconut-curry sauce. Totally oriental in aroma and flavor and served with totally Western fried yellow Finn potatoes.

For dessert, there are none of those vacuous, gelatinous Chinese concoctions, but Western creations. On my very first visit, I mistakenly deemed this sacriligious. For example, I shudder to think of chocolate (and me a chocoholic!) to cap off a Chinese meal. But then I tasted the lemon tart! Ah! such lip-pursing tartness, such smoothness. Barbara Tropp combines the best of both possible worlds in a unique cuisine that should not be missed.

Your Sixth Perfect Day Schedule

9:00 a.m. Easy on breakfast. It is going to be a long fun-
and food-filled day as we tour the beautiful
and historic wine country north of San
Francisco.

9:30 a.m. Drive across the majestic Golden Gate Bridge
to Sonoma and the Valley of the Moon.

10:30 a.m. Stroll around Sonoma's town square, visiting
handicraft shops and buildings dating from
California's colorful past.

12:00 noon Your options for lunch today include indulg-
ing in some Italian trattoria fare or picnicking
at either one of the state's loveliest and most
historic wineries or on the grounds of General
Vallejo's home.

2:00 p.m. Your tour of the wine country continues as
you leave the Valley of the Moon and cross the
hills into the famed Napa Valley.

3:45 p.m. Your final winery visit is the most spectacular
of all as an aerial tramway carries you to a hilltop complex overlooking the valley below.

6:00 p.m. On the way back to San Francisco, you have
your choice of dining in a uniquely San Francisco institution located in Marin County or
enjoying beautifully prepared old Cantonese
favorites.

The Sixth Day of Your
One Perfect Week in San Francisco

NOTE: Later on in this guide there is a recommended three-day trip to the Napa Valley, which covers some of the same area as this one-day outing. You may wish to refer to it, when making your plans for this shorter visit.

9:00 a.m.   Weather permitting, this full-day excursion can be the highlight of your San Francisco stay. (Even though it may be foggy in downtown San Francisco, chances are it will be sunny in the wine region.)

Featured are the scenic beauties of one of the world's richest wine-producing regions, glimpses of California's past and—naturally—some excellent wining and dining. However, it is a long day, so I advise starting now, perhaps fortified by a very light breakfast at your hotel.

9:30 a.m.   Drive out to Van Ness Avenue, a thorough-fare with which by now you should be well acquainted, and head north toward Lombard Street which leads onto the Golden Gate Bridge.

Approximately 20 miles along Highway 101 on the Marin County side, turn off onto Highway 37 (marked "Vallejo, Napa"). Seven and a half miles later, turn left onto Highway 121 (marked "Sonoma, Napa"), continuing for another 6 1/2 miles. Here, watch for signs leading to Sonoma, turning right and then left 1 mile later onto Highway 12.

By proceeding up Highway 12 (now called Broadway), in about four miles you will arrive at Sonoma's town square dominated by the old Sonoma City Hall, built in the Mission Revival Style early in this century.

This is the hub of your morning's itinerary. So find a parking space and we can begin our walking tour counter-clockwise around the square.

10:30 a.m.   Sonoma is a charming little town steeped in early California history. It is the home of the last California mission and for twenty-five days it was the capital of the Bear Flag Republic.

Back in the 1840s, American settlers braved all kind of hardships across endless miles of wilderness to reach California. But when they arrived, they found that the Mexican government, which controlled California, would not allow them to own land.

So in 1846, thirty settlers on horseback arrived in Sonoma at dawn, arrested the seemingly willing General Vallejo, the Mexican commandant, and declared California an independent republic. From unbleached muslin, and a contributed petticoat, a flag was fashioned with the words "California Republic" across the bottom. Above it was a simple drawing of a grizzly bear. Amidst cheers, this "Bear Flag" was hoisted up a flag pole in the plaza.

But the Bear Flag Republic did not last long. Because just 25 days later, an American ship captured Monterey, the Mexican capital of California, and claimed all of California for the United States. But even though the Bear Flag Republic lasted less than a month, we still have a constant reminder of its short but noble history. You see, in 1911 the State of California officially adopted the Bear Flag as its own state flag.

And in Sonoma today, we can see and visit the still-intact home of General Vallejo and even barracks which housed the Mexican soldiers under his command. Because luckily, before all visible vestiges of this colorful period of California's past had been eradicated, a movement was launched to preserve many of the historic buildings. Therefore, as you stroll around the square, it will not be too difficult to sense what this town was like in the 19th century.

However, not all the delights of Sonoma are of yesteryear. As in 1850 when people fled Gold Rush-crazed San Francisco for the calm of Sonoma's lovely valley, young artisans today are drawn to this unhassled, friendly town where they are keepers of small shops and handsome galleries in which you will find a wide variety of their handcrafted work. In addition, the town has a host of antique shops to attract both the browser and buyer.

But before I begin my browsing, I always stop by the Sonoma French Bakery, 470 First Street, next door to the movie theater. If not to buy, just to bask in the aroma. And don't be too surprised to find this tiny bakery jam-packed with a line extending onto the sidewalk. Why? Well, as any of those patient patrons will verify, this bakery turns out some of the finest sourdough French bread anywhere! How they do it, no one seems to know. Their other baked goods are often quite ordinary. But, the French bread. . . *c'est magnifique!* (By the way, since it is unavailable in San Francisco, any and all city friends would warmly welcome a loaf.)

Continue up First Street. On the far corner, you will find the old mission where, during the fall harvest, the grapes for the new vintage are blessed in a religious ceremony that has been conducted on this spot for nearly 150 years. Constructed in 1840, it is the last and northernmost of the 21 missions in California.

Now, turn left along Spain Street, the northern perimeter of the square. Here, you will find the barracks (1836-1840) which once housed General Vallejo's troops; plus a restored hotel from a later date. (For a very small entrance fee you can tour the barracks. And hold onto your ticket for it will also allow you admission to Vallejo's historical home.)

Further along Spain Street you will come upon the Sonoma Cheese Factory, 2 West Spain (open daily).

But before you go inside this home of Sonoma Jack cheese, let me ask what you would like to do for lunch... picnic at either a historic winery or Vallejo's home, or lunch at a hearty Italian trattoria right down the street?

While it may be too early to eat, you might want to decide now since the Sonoma Cheese Factory is an excellent provisions provider should a picnic interest you. Or if the town is hot and summer-season packed with visitors, and you would rather lunch indoors in an elegant trattoria, reservations should be made at Piatti.

If you still are unsure about what you want to do for lunch, don't flip a coin. Park yourself on the sidewalk bench out the Sonoma Cheese Factory and read ahead.

Picnicking in Sonoma is a favorite lunch option because not only are there two excellent—and both historic—picnic sites, but the Sonoma Cheese Factory has just about everything you will need, including some of that fabulous French bread from the Sonoma Bakery.

As one would assume in a cheese factory, great emphasis is placed upon cheese and you will find over 100 varieties. Be sure to ask for samples of some of their originals—Sonoma Cheddar and Sonoma Jack. (Through huge glass windows you can watch them actually make the cheese, while overhead a video explains the history and the process of Sonoma Jack Cheese.)

You can also buy beer here, but who would think of drinking that alien brew in California's beautiful wine country! Wine is the thing—with special emphasis on Sonoma Valley vintners such as Chateau St. Jean, Glen Ellen, Kenwood, Sebastiani, Smothers (yes, the TV brothers) and Gundlach-Bundschu. (A valley joke is that in order to pass a sobriety test a suspect driver must flawlessly pronounce Gundlach-Bundschu Gewurztraminer.)

If you wish to picnic at Vallejo's historic home (a short walk away), you should select a bottle congenial with your picnic selections. However, if you wish to picnic at my second locale recommendation—the historic Buena Vista Winery (a short drive away)—I think you'd have more fun if you waited and purchased your wine there, after tasting a few of their offerings.

Lachryma Montis, General Mariano Vallejo's home, is an easy half-mile walk from the plaza, provided the sun is not too intense. The name, which translates from the Latin into "Tears of the Mountain", refers to the artesian springs which fill a small reservoir on the twenty-acre property. And in a shaded arbor near the reservoir picnic tables await you.

The actual Vallejo home was not built until after the General had lost his position as the Mexican government's commandant of California. With California becoming part of the United States, the general left his Mexican-style Casa Grande on the plaza and built this classic two-story Gothic Revival house in 1851. And he lived here in this redwood-frame structure, with its large Gothic windows looking out onto orange and pomelo trees, until his death. The charming house, replete with Victorian furnishings brought around the Horn, is open to the public (a $1 charge).

To reach General Vallejo's home, simply turn right on exiting the Sonoma Cheese Company. Remain on Spain Street and in a few blocks a sign will direct you to turn right up an long entrance leading to the house. To return to the square, however, you may wish to turn left on a bicycle-walking path. This will take you past the Depot Museum. A right turn on East First Street, will take you back to the northeast corner of the plaza.

The grounds of the Buena Vista Winery, our alternative picnic site, are also rich in California history. For it was here that General Vallejo first planted grapes in 1832. But it was not until the arrival of a Hungarian nobleman, Count Agoston Haraszthy, that the Buena Vista was established as one of the first wineries in California.

After searching the West for over a decade in order to locate a suitable climate in which the grape-cuttings of his native Hungary would flourish, the Count discovered the Sonoma area or, as the Indians called it, the Valley of the Moon. Here he settled, striking up a close friendship-rivalry with General Vallejo (who was a proud amateur vintner) and by 1857, bottled his first pressings.

Because of his pioneering work in what is now one of California's most famous industries, Haraszthy has been officially recognized as "The Father of California Viticulture." The vine-covered stone building on your right dates from this early period of California's wine history. Stepping into its cool interior, you can take a short self-guided wine tour, which takes you back into the barrel-lined mountain-side cellars, dug by Chinese laborers over a century ago. In the tasting room, you may sample some of the Buena Vista's current output and purchase a bottle for your picnic at one of the tree-shaded tables overlooking a small stream opposite the winery.

To reach the Buena Vista Winery, drive east on Napa Street, the southern boundary of the town plaza. Continue on Napa Street until you cross some railroad tracks (about 1 mile), turning left immediately. However, no matter if you decided to lunch here, at General Vallejo's home or at Piatti, the Buena Vista Winery is a "must-see."

Piatti, 405 First Street West, Sonoma (707 996-2351; open daily for lunch and dinner; reservations advised), is the latest dining enterprise of Claude Rouas, owner of the deluxe Auberge du Soleil in the Napa Valley. Although M. Rouas is most certainly French—his brother Maurice is co-owner of that bastion of *haute cuisine*, Fleur de Lys in San Francisco—his current interests seem to be in the Italian manner. And right now, Italian cuisine leads the pack in trendiness.

Piatti is what I would call a trattoria—an informal place with greater emphasis on and greater success with pastas and appetizers. The dining room is in cool pastel shades, and the enclosed patio is forested with umbrellas to ward off the summer sun.

Fortunately, we will be visiting Piatti at lunch, because the most successful way to enjoy it is with an opener like prosciutto—either in the winter with greens or with a sweet summer melon. The quality of the Parma-style ham is superb—moist and not too overbearing in flavor. Or you might like slices of mozzarella—the soft, white Italian cheese. The carpaccio is fine razor-thin beef, but I am not a fan of the treatment which calls for sprinkling the dish with parmesan cheese shavings and capers. (Much more to my liking is the one presented at Acquerello in San Francisco, which you will find later in this guide.)

Pastas and especially risottos are what I really thrive on at Piatti. So be certain to ask about the rice of the day. On a recent outing, it was ideally cooked with that minuscule kernel of underdoneness in the center of each grain, yet the whole portion was creamy without being soupy. On this bright day, the rice was flavored with cheese, leeks and a whisper of fennel—delicious.

Also outstanding were wide, flat noodles (pappardelle) of pastel yellow (from saffron) which were introduced to a roast lamb and artichoke melange. In Firenze, pappardelle are classically treated to a rabbit ragout. But this was truly a noble pasta.

A light and quite successful main course—if you wish to go further—are the grilled vegetables served with grilled polenta triangles. But a veal liver alla Trevisana was extremely dark and too cumbersome for a warm afternoon. The beef steak fiorentina was adequate, but nothing like one you would have at, for example, Celestina, my favorite beefsteakery in that exquisite Tuscan city.

Unfortunately, the Italian ices—ideal on hot days—tend to be too sugar-intense for my taste. But a tiramisu—the wonderous confection of lady fingers, mascarpone cheese and chocolate—is excellent.

The wine list, as in all Sonoma restaurants of any repute, is ample. However, if you order an ordinary red—say the "house red" or something in that class—you drink from thick water glasses. A finer and more costly California white, however, produces tall blue-stemmed glasses in keeping with the elegance of the wine. Now that's Italian!

2:00 p.m.   Time to tear yourself away from either Piatti's lip-smacking risotto or your picnic spread. From the Buena Vista, simply drive back to the Sonoma town square. From Piatti just walk out the front door.

Now then, you should leave Sonoma by driving west out Napa Street, the square's southern perimeter. Following the Highway 12 markers toward Santa Rosa, you will soon pass through small towns such as Boyes Hot Springs, Fetters Hot Springs and Agua Caliente, names harkening back to when this area supported many spas, fed by hot mineral springs from the nearby mountains.

While this area has little grace or charm now—seedy is

the word that comes immediately to mind—you will pass on your left the Sonoma Mission Inn, an elegant modern spa.

Six and a half miles after turning off Napa Street, keep a careful eye open for a sign indicating "Trinity Road—Oakville." Turn right here and almost instantly you will find yourself climbing a ridge of mountains with over-the-shoulder views of the Valley of the Moon behind you.

Remain on this road, following the signs to the Oakville Grade, and you will abruptly top the crest. Before you, in sweeping panorama, lies the fertile Napa Valley.

Visitors who have never toured wine-producing areas are often shocked to discover that in late fall, grape leaves turn into the flaming red, deep orange, and purple of New England's fall foliage. Should this be the time of your visit, this view is all the more awesome.

Proceed down the grade to Highway 29, turn left and you are in the very heart of the great Napa Valley. For the next several miles you will be passing what reads like a *Who's Who* of old California winemakers—Beaulieu, Inglenook, Robert Mondavi, Beringer, Charles Krug—all with tasting rooms!

I can remember years ago, when these were just about the only California wines. Today, every time I open a wine list, I come across a new boutique winery's output. It makes wine-tasting in California an avocation unto itself!

In order to weed out the Sunday imbiber from the more serious wine taster-purchaser, many wineries have been forced to insist visitors take a tour prior to entering the tasting room. Therefore, the number of wineries you visit and how much wine you sample is up to you. But watch the clock. Our last scheduled winery is Sterling Vineyards, 1 mile south of Calistoga off Highway 29. Another "must see." And it closes at 4:30 p.m. which means you should arrive there about 4:00 p.m.

3:45 p.m.   Well, time to head further north to the far end of the Napa Valley and Sterling Vineyards. After passing through beautiful St. Helena, with some graceful old mansions on the left, and just after the sign to the Napa Valley State Park, start watching for a cluster of white buildings on a hilltop to your right.

Once in sight, you may think that somehow the stark white structures of an Aegean Island have been magically transported to a California landscape. (Camera buffs take note: You will be leaving the winery via a different route. Therefore, this unique view will not come again.)

Just when you think you have missed the turnoff, you will see a sign indicating "Dunaweal Lane, to Sterling Vineyards" and others directing you to the visitors' parking area. Here, at the hill's base, is an aerial tramway which will silently carry you up to the winery for a $5.00 per person charge.

It is worth every cent. For at the summit, you can conduct yourself through one of the most beautiful wineries in the state. Actually, the interior is comparable to a contemporary museum with ancient and modern art depicting all phases of wine-making. Each step of the process is clearly explained and the actual machinery is visible.

Yet, not even this impressive tour can compete with the vista of the surrounding lush valley. I have intentionally scheduled your arrival here late in the day when most of the visitors have departed. At this more quiet time, the winery takes on a monastic air. And when the many bells—originally from St. Dunstan's Church in London—peel out from their towers, it is a moment to remember.

Naturally, wine tastings are available in a handsome lounge or on a sunny patio. But before you enter the tasting area, be sure to visit the "Chai" for a moment. This is a remarkably beautiful chapel-like sanctum where precious older wines quietly and gracefully age. The modern stained-glass window gloriously celebrates the colors of wine. (Out-of-staters can be somewhat frustrated if they become attached to Sterling wines as they are difficult to locate in most liquor stores. Sterling prefers to reserve much of their output for purchases at the winery and for diners in finer restaurants.)

6:00 p.m.   Well, time to leave the tranquility of this marvelous white aerie, and press on. So glide back to the valley floor via the tramway and exit from the winery.

This ends our day's outing. However, if you do not mind undertaking the hour drive back to San Francisco after dinner you can dine superbly right here in the Napa Valley. Back in St. Helena there are two excellent restaurants—Trilogy and Terra—and further homeward in Yountville is Mustards, one of the best grills in Northern California. For full descriptions of all three of these notable restaurants, please see the section entitled "A Three Day Trip to the Napa Valley" further on in this book.

However, if you are driving directly back to San Francisco, turn right on exiting Sterling Winery. Soon, another right will head you back down the Napa Valley, not on Highway 29 but rather on the lesser traveled Silverado Trail.

Since all the wineries are now closed, I prefer to use the less trafficked Silverado Trail for this portion of my return to San Francisco. Being a less commercial route, you are closer to the beauty of the vineyards around you.

Simply continue down the Silverado Trail until it deadends at Trancas Street in Napa. Turn right for 2 miles, then left onto Highway 29 (marked "Vallejo"). Now follow Highway 121 signs which will lead you into Highway 37. Highway 37 will lead you directly to Highway 101 south to San Francisco, which is the route we started north on this morning.

While traveling back to San Francisco, you might wish to consider having dinner at one of two restaurants, purposely included in today's schedule for some very important reasons: both offer excellent, comfortable food; both are easily accessible from the route you must take to reach downtown San Francisco (no need to change your clothes, casual attire perfectly acceptable); neither accepts reservations. Therefore, you will not have to worry about arriving at a set time; and both offer a simplicity which would ideally cap this long day.

Marin Joe's, 1585 Casa Buena Drive off Highway 101, Corte Madera (924-2081; open nightly for dinner and for lunch weekdays), is one of a special breed of restaurants native to San Francisco.

To any resident, a "Joe's" restaurant immediately means an open charcoal grill, a heavily Italian-accented menu with equal emphasis on steaks and chops, and counter as well as booth service. San Francisco still boasts several Joe's, yet today, the mantle of "top Joe's" rests securely on the shoulders of this Marin County roadside operation.

Here, frozen vegetables are shunned (except for an occasional appearance in the mixed-vegetable garnish) and shortcuts, such as powdered stock concentrates in the minestrone, are abhorred. What you find is good wholesome, down-to-earth cooking, expertly done by a team of chefs who work with dazzling elan. Their performance is best witnessed from a ringside counter seat.

Start with a cup or bowl of Marin Joe's fine minestrone, followed by either a rib steak (that old-fashioned, deliciously juicy cut now making a well deserved reappearance on restaurant menus) or their extra-thick lamb chops (medium rare, of course). Naturally, be certain you specify your steak or chops be charcoal broiled. The pastas are also quite fine but you must request that they be cooked to order, *al dente*, for which you pay a slight premium.

Side orders of vegetables play important roles in any Joe's meal, especially at Marin Joe's where they are fresh. Therefore, I always ask that the mixed vegetables which come with the meat courses be replaced (at a slight charge) by either Swiss chard, Italian beans, zucchini or spinach. All these vegetables have been parboiled in advance. However, each order is sauteed to order in olive oil with a touch of garlic, arriving at your table piping hot and delicious.

One dish that every Joe's and only a Joe's features is the Joe's Special. Legend has it that late one night many years ago, a group of regulars arrived at a Joe's to find the kitchen's food supply almost depleted. All the chef could stir up were some eggs, ground beef, onions and leftover parboiled spinach. Well, stir them up he did, scrambling them into a concoction that is neither scrambled eggs nor omelette but strictly San Franciscan! On request, Marin Joe's will add fresh sliced mushrooms for an elegant touch.

Desserts are almost non-existent except for a sensational zabaione, that frothy Italian delight of whipped eggs and Marsala wine. I prefer Marin Joe's version to any in San Francisco's far more deluxe and expensive restaurants. But then, quality takes center stage here, not elaborate service or fancified decor.

Oh yes, should you happen to find yourself in Marin county on a Monday noon, run—do not walk—to Marin Joe's. For on that day they serve freshly made polenta. And it's like Mama made, if she happened to be born in Northern Italy. And when ordering it, ask if they could serve it with some slightly underdone liver in the Venetian style, instead of the usual veal stew. It's my favorite Marin County lunch!

To reach Marin Joe's, as you drive south towards San Francisco on Highway 101, after San Rafael start watching for a turnoff to the right marked "Paradise Dr./Tamalpais Dr." Take this exit and proceed to the right to the second stoplight, keeping to the far left. Turn left onto Casa Buena which runs parallel to the freeway. Marin Joe's is on the right around the curve past the Cadillac dealership. You can't miss it; there will be a hundred cars parked outside!

After dinner, all you need do to reach San Francisco is continue south on Casa Buena and in a minute, you will be able to re-enter the freeway, heading to the Golden Gate Bridge, San Francisco and your hotel.

Another dinner suggestion is: Mike's Chinese Cuisine, 5145 Geary Boulevard at 16th Avenue (752-0120; dinners served nightly except Tuesdays). Mike's is a nice, comfortable Chinese restaurant. Not just comfortable in its pleasant surroundings but comfortable in its menu. Because this is a bastion of those Chinese dishes we all grew up on. No fierce Szechwan spiciness, no exotic sea snails. Just classic Cantonese dishes, extremely well prepared.

And there are two aspects of Mike's that make dinner here usually especially rewarding. Unlike all too many Chinatown places which continue to add more and more inexpensive ingredients—such as huge chunks of celery, onion and bamboo, to stretch dishes and keep costs down—Mike's does not hesitate in raising prices while keeping the quality pristine. And, whereas the rotation of chefs in large establishments, especially those open for lunch and dinner, often makes Chinese dining a variation of Russian roulette, at Mike's, Mike is personally in the kitchen just about every night and therefore, the consistency is practically unfailing.

Mike's style of clear, unencumbered cooking is apparent in my perennial first course, a mustard green soup—sparkling clear broth, brilliantly green under-done mustard greens, tender filets of pork and a shred of ginger. The delicate sweetness of the stock and tender pork contrasted with the quasi-bitterness of the mustard greens represents, to me, the quintessence of Cantonese cuisine. My second course is usually the chicken salad, that compelling mixture of shredded chicken, lettuce, coriander and onions.

Then, if you fancy sweet and sour pork, meet the San Francisco champion: sweet and sour pork deluxe. Cubes of tender pork, batter-dipped and fried to the proper outer crispness, are bathed in a luxuriant sauce rich with translucent pieces of preserved melon, pineapple cubes, and gingery delicacies. The paper-wrapped chicken is another favorite, while the crystal shrimp (quickly stir-fried so they all but explode in your mouth) are excellent. If, like me, you simply cannot get enough of the refreshing clean flavors of Chinese vegetables, then try the tenderloin with chinese greens, or the beef with sugar pea pods.

End your dinner, as most Chinese would, with a stellar steamed rock cod, its silk-smooth sweet flakes gently flavored by ginger, onion, coriander and soy sauce. That should ring down the curtain on a great Cantonese dinner! And should you return here next year, you would find the exact same menu, the same undulled freshness, the same expert flavor balance, and stylistic simplicity. That's

Mike's—a reassuringly comfortable Chinese restaurant of the old school. Moderate prices.

How to reach Mike's? Cross the Golden Gate Bridge into San Francisco. A few hundred yards past the toll plaza, curve to the right following the signs to 19th Avenue (Highway 1). After a short tunnel, you will be on Park-Presidio Drive. At the fourth stoplight (Geary Street), turn right for two blocks and you will find Mike's on the left-hand side of the street. After dinner, all you need do is head down Geary in the opposite direction from which you arrived. Geary will take you directly downtown.

10:30 p.m.   Well, whether you dined at Marin Joe's or Mike's Chinese Cuisine, you now should be back at your hotel probably just as bushed as I am. However, if you're not (bushed, that is), all I can say is any carousing you want to do after a day like this will have to be done on your own! Good night. See you tomorrow.

Your Seventh Perfect Day Schedule

9:00 a.m. Time only for a quick coffee before you launch your last day in San Francisco.

10:45 a.m. Either tie up all those last-day loose ends or relax aboard a cruise ship and tour the Bay, seeing San Francisco from an exciting, different perspective.

12:00 noon Enjoy a buffet high atop a Nob Hill tower with a 360-degree view of the Bay or lunch in a crowded financial-district "find".

2:00 p.m. It's a free afternoon. Enjoy it by revisiting and resavoring your favorite corner of San Francisco; drop in on a museum of photography; or take a hike!

6:30 p.m. With the city at your feet, sip a farewell cocktail in one of our high-in-the-sky rooms.

8:00 p.m. A final elegant dinner in either the city's most venerable dining room... in a bastion of French cuisine seldom discovered by tourists... or in an old North Beach joint that made a top-10 list—for rudest in the nation!

10:30 p.m. If you are heading home tomorrow morning, or are setting out on one of the exciting side trips detailed in Part Two of this book, you had better call it an evening. So until we meet in San Francisco again, *au revoir, auf Wiedersehen, arrivederci*—so long.

The Seventh Day of Your

One Perfect Week in San Francisco

9:00 a.m.   Good morning! Well, this could be your last full day in San Francisco. Therefore, I purposely have framed a very loose format for you today. I know that whenever I enjoy a week or more in any one city, I invariably find that on my last day, there are many loose ends to take care of, such as returning the rental car, picking up purchases held at stores, firing off a few last postcards, etc. Also, there are favored places to revisit, to resavor before leaving. Or some new ones to discover. And for you, today is that last day to fit it all in.

So since it is going to be a busy day—with a good-sized lunch—why don't we just get moving after a quick cup of coffee?

For those of you who have tied up all those loose ends and wish to experience another facet of San Francisco this morning, I am not about to abandon you. Why not enjoy your last perfect morning in San Francisco on San Francisco Bay?

10:45 a.m.   Hard by Fisherman's Wharf you will come upon a ship of the Red & White Fleet (546-2800; ships depart from either Pier 41 or nearby Pier 43 1/2) ready to take you aboard for a 45-minute cruise of the Bay.

These cruise ships depart as early as 10:45 a.m. daily from March through September at one hour and fifteen minute intervals, but on weekends only during the winter.

On board and under way, you will turn westward toward the Golden Gate. From either the warmth of the enclosed lower deck or from the breeze-swept top deck, you can watch San Francisco's skyline pass in review.

First, Fisherman's Wharf with Russian Hill in the background; then Fort Mason and the Marina with its row of luxury homes overlooking the yacht harbor. A taped narration, happily bereft of those lame puns and stale jokes which afflict most tour talks, will call your attention to points of interest ashore.

You will be acquainted with many of the landmarks, such as the Palace of Fine Arts and Fort Point, having already visited them earlier in your stay. But the Bay cruise places them in a different, overall perspective, set against the backdrop of the city's hills and, hopefully, a brilliant blue sky.

Soon, your ship will timidly poke its prow under the Golden Gate Bridge, gracefully arching high overhead, and hastily turn back from the choppy waters of the entrance to the smoother Bay itself. Within a few minutes, you will be gliding by Alcatraz, now deserted except for bands of curious visitors traipsing through the vacant cell blocks.

On the port side, you will see Treasure Island, site of the 1939 World's Fair and now a U.S. Navy base. If some of the buildings appear a bit grandiose for a naval installation, it is just that they are remnants of the Fair's exotic architecture.

And then it's back to Fisherman's Wharf with the exciting skyline of downtown San Francisco towering high above in the background. It is a marvelously impressive sight.

(By the way, the ships of the Red & White Fleet are available for charter. Each can accommodate from 50 to 500 passengers and can depart from one of several San Francisco, East Bay and Marin County docks.)

12:00 noon. By now you will have docked at Fisherman's Wharf. And unless you wish to revisit The Cannery or Ghirardelli Square, I suggest you head to your luncheon spot.

My two recommendations are as different as can be! One is not noted for its cuisine, but rather for its 360-degree view of San Francisco. The other, located on the edge of the financial district, offers a happy selection of dishes in a bar atmosphere alive with the banging of San Francisco's perennial luncheon pastime, liar's dice.

The Crown Room, Fairmont Hotel, Mason and California Streets (772-5131; buffet lunch served daily), is perched on the very top of the Fairmont Hotel Tower high atop Nob Hill. Yet aside from its awesome view it offers luncheon goers probably the most impressive buffet in town.

Actually, buffets can be the bane of any food critic's life. It has become painfully apparent that the vast majority of chefs who prepare buffets are seriously infected by the "dazzle them with quantity" virus and are totally impervious to the "it's quality, not quantity" antidote.

The most noticeable talent these so-called chefs display is their ability to operate a can opener, as evidenced by endless bowls of canned fruit, assorted olives and artless tuna salads. I, therefore, usually avoid buffets like the plague!

Luckily for you, however, the Crown Room buffet is a noteworthy exception. First of all, this buffet is extremely high on fresh, top-quality ingredients. Gleaming bowls of fresh papaya, pineapple, berries in season, etc., greet you. Secondly, there is no skimping on the more costly foods. Copious platters of pates, delicate bay shrimp and even poached fresh salmon, when in season, are often part of the lavish display.

And when the more ubiquitous buffet fare, such as pickled beets, cucumber salad, chicken salad, etc., are used, each is touched with creativity by intriguing vinaigrettes or sauces, or mixed in palate-pleasing combinations which offer a parade of delightful flavors and textures.

On the other hand, the Crown Room's chef is only slightly more successful than most buffet builders when it comes to presenting hot selections. I suppose it is asking too much of them to come up with hot dishes capable of withstanding the steam table's debilitating environment.

Even though some of these hot dishes can appear above average, I approach them with skepticism, concentrating on the superior cold offerings. Pastries are nice, but not

Oscar winning. All in all, the excellence and variety of the buffet's cold dishes, combined with the breathtaking view, make the Crown Room a rare and delightful experience. Expensive.

If you decide to lunch at the Crown Room the best way to reach it from the Bay Cruise dock is by cable car. You'll find the Fisherman's Wharf terminal for the Powell Street line at Bay and Taylor Streets, just a few blocks from the pier. So hop on for your last ride and simply hop off at the Fairmont Hotel. Also, be sure to take the outside elevator up to the Crown Room. You'll love the way the Bay panorama unfolds as you climb higher and higher.

Eddie Rickenbacker's, 133 Second Street near Mission (543-3498; lunch served Monday through Friday; dinner nightly except Sunday; reservations best), looks like it's been here for years. But actually this bar *cum* food opened only in 1987. And instantly it became popular as a local's lunch hangout.

You will note, for example, the phone is in a completely enclosed booth. Probably not because brokers don't want luncheoners to eavesdrop on their latest tip, but because lawyers calling in to report that they are still tied up in court will not have their alibis ruined by the incessant banging of liar's dice at the huge bar.

Until October of 1989, the decor—if you can call it such—was dominated by an real vintage Sopwith Camel fighter plane suspended from the ceiling. Then, so I am told, the owner lost it in a dice game at the bar one night. But, philosophized the waiter who told me this typically San Francisco tale, that might have been best. Because just two nights after the World War I fighter plane had been removed, the October 17 tremblor hit. "And who knows," the waiter said "had it still been up there, someone might have been wearing it!"

My lunch opens at Eddie's with a negroni—equal parts of Campari, gin and sweet vermouth. Then if I am really ravenous, I order one of their wonderful Caesar salads, as lovely to look as it is to devour. The picture-perfect romaine leaves are obviously tossed with a creamy garlic-scented vinaigrette, dusted with grated cheese and then reformed into what looks like a large open blossom. The mixed green salad—featuring several different greens—is accorded equal attention. These are two of the best salads in town.

The daily soup displays some of the kitchen's finest attributes. For example, a minestrone, chock-a-block with slightly underdone zucchini and spiked with pesto. Or a concoction of spicy Mexican sausage, lima beans, pancetta and tomato all in a rich creamy stock. Preceded by a salad, these meal-in-a-bowl soups make ideal lunches.

If you wish a heartier lunch, their rib-eye steak is exemplary. There is also a novel dish of sliced Black Forest ham with correctly boiled and marinated new potatoes all under a blanket of melted fontina cheese. There is always a daily fresh fish—for example, a delicious halibut steak flavored with a discreet basil-aioli butter—often served with slightly crunchy julienned vegetables. I tend to shy away from their pastas, which can be variable. The excellent quality, course-ground hamburgers are served on thick sourdough buns, which would make them a challenge for even Martha Raye!

Desserts are also ample in size. But when they are as good as the bourbon-laced pecan pie, that is not a complaint! There is also a flourless, pudding-like Italian walnut-chocolate cake, pushed over the calorie-counter edge by a warm fudge sauce and whipped cream. But live it up, it's your last day in San Francisco.

2:00 p.m.   I have nothing specific planned for you this afternoon. As the tour brochures would say, it is a "free afternoon." Perhaps you want to fill it by revisiting your favorite San Francisco places, by strolling through Chinatown once again, by dropping in at that museum which you just didn't have enough time for, by sitting contentedly in Golden Gate Park and soaking in its beauty and freedom.

But if you would like a few more suggestions, I do have a few totally diverse ones.

One is to experience the ultimate in urban environments by strolling through the Embarcadero Center. Here, in an area just west of the Ferry Building, on the site of what was once San Francisco's produce markets, loom the flat, grey, sky-reaching towers of what many natives originally called with great disdain Manhattan West, the Embarcadero Center.

However, I believe that secretly many San Franciscans rather relished watching these steel and concrete monoliths rise, imparting to the city's skyline a far more dramatic profile.

During the day, the Center is ant-hill alive with thousands of office workers who do not even have to touch street level (walk-overs interconnect the massive structures) to shop, lunch or sun in the flower-festooned open spaces. But at night, the Center is almost deserted, even though its many restaurants lure diners with the welcome of free indoor parking, etc.

On a moonlit night, with its giant steel sculptures agleam, you can get the eerie impression you have been transported to some mysteriously abandoned world of tomorrow.

While browsing through the mall-like Center, you might wish to do a bit more shopping with an eye towards finding something to take home with you as a suitable memento of your San Francisco stay. . . something that will recapture for you the look and feel of the city. Why not drop into a bookstore and ask for a copy of *Above San Francisco, Volume II*, published by Cameron & Company?

This breathtaking volume of color photographs presents San Francisco in all her glory as seen by a swooping gull or jet pilot. Dazzlingly photographed from above, in a clarity which rivals that rare light of the Aegean Islands, this is San Francisco as we who live here like to think of her. . .and as we hope you will remember her.

Another suggestion, especially if you are interested in the art of photography is to visit The Ansel Adams Center, 250 Fourth Street across from Moscone Hall (495-7000; open daily except Monday).

Run by the Friends of Photography, this latest of San Francisco museums celebrates the genius of arguably America's greatest photographer, Ansel Adams, in a rotating exhibit in one of its five galleries. In the others, you will find the entire spectrum of photography from historic photos to the most avant-garde montages.

My other suggestion—also of great interest to camera buffs—is to personally view and photograph San Francisco from an incredibly dramatic viewpoint, a virtual photographer's paradise.

No, I am not suggesting you take a helicopter ride over the Bay, although they are available, but rather that you take a hike in the hills of Marin. So after donning sensible shoes (the hike is not arduous), we can go off to Marin by bus.

On Van Ness Avenue, at either Geary, Sutter, Clay or Union Street, you can catch a Golden Gate Transit bus (for information call 332-6600) that will in about 15 minutes take you across the Golden Gate Bridge and into Marin County. (On boarding the bus, make certain it stops at Spencer Avenue above Sausalito; as of this moment the #20, #60, #70 and #80 all do so.)

On leaving the bus at Spencer Avenue continue along the frontage road for a few hundred yards, until you reach an underpass on your left. Walk through the underpass and you will see immediately ahead trail markers indicating the trail head.

The initial 15 minutes is up a steep trail, part staircase, cut into the hillside. But take your time. At each turning, new views of the Bay open up, while the eucalyptus groves through which you pass always sustain some wildflowers.

At the top, turn left. When you reach a paved road, a sign will indicate a trail on the right, which you should follow in the direction of San Francisco. Here the going is easy, along an almost level trail that cuts across the hillside covered with a host of wildflowers. You might even spot some grazing deer.

Off on your right is the Pacific Ocean. And then as you round first one bend then another, the vast vista of San Francisco emerges, piece by piece.

If you hike out far enough, you will come to one of the great dream spots favored by both amateur and commercial photographers ever since the Golden Gate Bridge was built. For you will actually be above the tops of the bridge's towers. And beyond them lies the entire city of San Francisco, stretching from Bay to Ocean Beach. I know of no comparable view—anywhere!

Once you have your fill of this magnificent spectacle, simply retrace your route, back down the trail-stairs to the highway. And right there, within a few yards of the last step, is the passenger shelter from where you can board a San Francisco-bound bus (departures at thirty-minute intervals).

Crossing the Golden Gate for the last time, you will have time to think back on your visit. And perhaps, if you have fallen in love with her as much as the writers of these words, you might consider just "What is San Francisco?" I hope you won't mind, if I add my thoughts.

Countless columnists and authors have mulled over the question for years and the library is packed with their varied conclusions. There are even entire books devoted to the subject. To follow in the wake of such illustrious company is daring, but I do not feel this book would be complete without my attempt.

To understand the lure and charm of San Francisco, we must first destroy a myth. That myth is the notion that San Francisco is a "second New York." Nothing could be further from the truth.

San Francisco and New York are completely different. For sheer facilities, art museums, theaters, restaurants, and every other diversion, there is no city in America to compete with New York. However, San Francisco, while offering a somewhat lesser variety of these diversions, does make them more accessible to everyone. And when you add to that its charm, its less frantic pace, its bayside beauty and its generally benign weather, then San Francisco has no peer.

It is impossible to answer the question, "What is San Francisco?" without falling into a kind of flowery, self-conscious prose which defeats its own purpose. I have never read a good description of San Francisco. And not wishing to follow failure with failure, I will attempt to answer the question, "What is San Francisco?" by simply summing up the city's outstanding points.

San Francisco is in the unique and fortunate position of offering its residents and visitors many of the facilities of a great metropolis without forcing them to sacrifice their natural love of greenery and fresh air. It is a city of views, of shiny leaves, of sunsets, of water, of green earth.

In New York City, for instance, it is quite possible to live in Brooklyn or Queens and to travel back and forth to work in Manhattan by subway and never, except by chance, see any expanse of water or groves of trees. Not so in San Francisco.

The very heart of the shopping district on Market Street provides one with a clear view of Twin Peaks. From the top of elegant Nob Hill, the East Bay and rural Marin County can be easily seen. And as this little quick trek to the Marin headlands has demonstrated, in just moments you can be out in the country, amidst wildflowers and deer.

And as major cities go, San Francisco is relatively uncrowded. On the downtown hub's busiest day, the Friday after Thanksgiving Day, the crowds are no more dense than on an average day along New York's Fifth Avenue.

And perhaps it is this less frantic environment with fewer annoyances than are encountered in other large metropolitan areas, that allows San Franciscans to lighten up, to not take themselves too seriously! Although civic pride is never in short supply, we like nothing better than to kid our city, its officials, and most of all—ourselves.

I've always believed that part of the lightness of San Francisco, its easier life style, may be a partial reflection of the city's actual physical color. For basically San Francisco is a white city.

That becomes most obvious when you view it from the vantage point of the Marin headlands. Not only its skyscrapers but most of its homes are light in color, and, particularly on a sunny day, have a just-scrubbed look about them which continually gives the city a fresh youthful character.

And I believe that since all the above traits contribute to a less hectic, less harassed life, San Franciscans have the time to be more courteous. We take almost a civic pride in our day-to-day courtesy. There are exceptions, of course. But by and large, restaurant personnel, clerks, even bus drivers, and especially the wonderful breed of cable-car gripmen dispense courteous treatment freely to the public. Simply purchasing a loaf of bread in a busy bakery will often find kind words or small talk exchanged between customer and clerk.

Will it last? Will the uniqueness and individuality of San Francisco last? I certainly hope so. Nevertheless, every day brings change. Real estate interests have physically altered the face of downtown San Francisco almost beyond recognition from a few decades ago.

For example, it was not that long ago when Bush Street gave you a full view of the Bay. Now you look into a wall of glass and steel. Every day small, individual shops and restaurants give up the ghost, because escalating rents force them out. And usually they are replaced by the commonplace corporate.

So while the city which I hope you enjoyed this week is not at all the same as it was even fifteen years ago, I believe the intangible San Francisco is changing far more slowly. Because whether we be native or newcomer, we feel we are San Franciscans and are a part of something very, very special.

6:30 p.m.   Where will it be for cocktails this evening? Perhaps a return to the Top of the Mark to watch it grow dark, or another go around of the Equinox Room, or maybe you would like to sample a different room-with-a-view, the one high atop the St. Francis Hotel Tower (right on Union Square) called Victor's.

A high-powered outside elevator propels you above Union Square in a matter of seconds. Once seated in one of the semi-secluded alcoves, you can gaze out over the entire downtown area, the Bay and the East Bay hills beyond. Whichever view room you choose, the city lying at your feet will now, I hope, seem a very familiar place, filled with a great many memories to cherish.

8:00 p.m. If it was difficult for me to select from among all our great restaurants the ones to offer you on your First Perfect Day, the choice is equally challenging for tonight. Not only do I want to provide you with fine cuisine, but also the appropriate atmosphere for that true San Francisco finale.

In addition, while the three I have decided upon range in price from moderate to expensive, their greatest contrast lies in their approaches to dining out in San Francisco.

Caffe Sport, 574 Green (981-1251; lunch and dinner daily except Sunday and Monday; reservations essential; *cash only*), once made a national top-ten list—as one of the rudest restaurants in America. And I will not argue the point. But, especially if you have a party of four or six, it is also one of the city's most notorious "fun" places, that just so happens to serve totally delicious Sicilian cooking.

When you call for a reservation, you will be asked which of the two nightly seatings you wish. And when you accept one, you had better be there—*out front* of the tiny North Beach operation on time! Because when your name is called, should you not respond chances are your reservation will be immediately cancelled.

The interior looks like a bizarre junk shop. From the ceiling hangs a profusion of brilliantly colored little Sicilian carriages, garlands of garlic (which you had better love, if you dine here!), wine bottles, and just plain junk. There is not a square inch that is left undecorated.

The booth I was last in was backed by what at first glance appeared to be small antique murals. When I examined them closer, I found they were cheap Norman Rockwell reproductions which had been glazed over and set into the mosaic of the wall.

Seating in problematic. "Move over," hollered the T-shirted waiter, since three more diners were to join us at our already elbow-to-elbow table. And maybe—just maybe—while you wait for the place to fill up (which it does nightly) you might be able to con a bottle of Pinot Grigio out of a waiter.

When there is no more room at any of the tables, almost illegible sheets of photocopy are tossed onto the tables— the menu. And while you scan the fifteen or so items, you must understand how food is served at the Caffe Sport.

For starters, you and your guests must decide on communal dishes. None of this, "I'll have linguine and she'll have penne and he'll have. . ." No way! Your party decides on which dishes they want for the table, not individually.

Also, if they are out of a listed item, as you order it, the waiter will wearily shake his head until you hit on something they do have. Or he will simply say take this or that. And that's what you'll take.

After all orders are placed, cutlery, paper napkins and plates arrive—the latter often slid across the huge tables— with the admonition, "Don't break the fine china!" Only an atomic meltdown could possibly put a dent into these hard plastic discs.

Well then, you might be wondering, why do diners jam the joint nightly? Are they all members of the San Francisco Masochists Society? No, they are simply hooked on the truly superb, peasanty Sicilian food that will start pouring out of the kitchen doors in a minute. And if you have the right attitude, the rudeness, the noise, the hustle, all becomes theater.

What to order? Well, Caffe Sport is basically a seafood restaurant so you will find almost no meat on the menu— except perhaps in a pasta sauce. But in the confines of communal ordering, there are no individually prepared fish courses.

I always dive into this food fest with a pasta—invariably penne. And if you like pesto—that glorious Genovese blend of basil, garlic and cheese, perhaps studded with pine nuts—then you have hit pay dirt. The pasta will be precisely cooked—apparently the entire seating's pasta is cooked right before serving—and tossed with the dreamy green sauce. If you don't like too much grated cheese on top, be ready to stay the waiter's overliberal hand.

Then I usually have another course: a mammoth platter of eggplant (melanzane) in a tomato sauce and covered with melted cheese.

For a main course, I cannot miss the prawns all'Antonio, deliciously sweet and bathed in a garlicky white sauce which is lavished over slices of some green fresh vegetable, asparagus or zucchini. The same melange can also be ordered over pasta. You will sop up every morsel, but pay dearly tomorrow by reeking of garlic. (There is an old wives' tale that San Franciscans are immune to fleas, which can thrive in our dry summers, because of the vast quantities of garlic we consume.)

And really that's about it. After paying in cash only, you will leave Caffe Sport contented and probably laughing merrily as you recount all the "Did you see what happened when. . ." stories. Even in a city renowned for its unusual dining spots, Caffe Sport is unique.

Jack's, 615 Sacramento Street near Montgomery (986-9854; open nightly for dinner and for lunch Monday through Friday; reservations advised; *no credit cards*), is a cherished San Francisco institution of over a century and a quarter.

The great-great-grandchildren of our founding families today dine at their ancestral tables, greeting the tuxedoed waiters familiarly, as though they were old family retainers. The decor is men's room lighting and plastic palms. Tables are set with thick dishes you would never call china.

As for the cuisine at Jack's, it is staunchly old-fashioned, simple, unfrilly French. I doubt if a morsel of goat cheese, a kiwi slice or a single green peppercorn has ever sullied a plate. I can personally attest to the menu being unchanged for the thirty years I have been frequenting Jack's. This single sheet of paper, printed daily, contains such throwbacks as mammoth ripe olives and celery en branch as hors d'oeuvres and English mutton chops and broiled Salisbury steak for entrees.

There are a couple of daily soups. If it's the sorrel, do not miss it. Because you will be served an unadorned—no cunningly clever floats of chile, etc.—but flavorful, hearty soup like the kind a good French provincial housewife would have ladled out to her family fifty years ago. I find it ambrosial.

If it is crab season, I can never pass up their sauteed crab legs served with an excellent sauce Bearnaise. But that is about as fancy as I venture at Jack's

Their simple unsauced fish, such as the infinitely fragile sand dabs, are outstanding. And I often split an order as a first course. But for a main cause I can hardly be swayed from their rack of lamb for two—nice and underdone, and served with oniony potatoes boulangere—an unbeatable combination.

With it try a side order (everything is strictly a la carte with only a sprinkle of chopped parsley as garnish) of their spectacular deep-fried eggplant. When they arrive they will probably look horrible—odd-sized pieces fried to a dark brown. But inside: molten eggplant. Delicious.

For dessert: any fresh berries or melon in season; or their simple French pancakes, not the fancily flamed ones known as Suzettes, but just ordinary little crepes, sprinkled with granulated sugar. The coffee, served in thick lunchroom crockery, is totally forgettable. Nevertheless, if I were forced into exile and had to leave my beloved San Francisco, my last meal would be the above described feast—not only because it is delicious, but because it is served at Jack's.

Le Castel, 3235 Sacramento Street (921-7115; dinners served nightly except Sunday; reservations a must), is regarded as one of San Francisco's finest quietly elegant French restaurants. Yet, relatively few visitors find their way to this stylishly redone residence out near Presidio Avenue. Why? Well, Le Castel has eschewed the kind of tourist-enticing publicity ploys practiced by so many more well-known restaurants.

Instead, owner Fritz Frankel has quietly developed a limited yet remarkably interesting menu, primarily based on Alsatian-accented French classic cuisine in a style reminiscent of a fine old Parisian establishment.

With it he has earned for Le Castel the loyalty of a large and devoted local clientele, among whom I am happy to include myself.

Where to begin? Well, if you relish brains, you cannot afford to miss the calf's brains in black butter. Their custardy texture is perfectly preserved and their dulcet flavor is ideally framed by the nut-like browned butter and the accent of capers. Or a magnificent fish mousse—of fresh halibut, for example—wearing a spinach cap and surrounded by an aristocratic *beurre blanc*. Then there might be a confit of duck served over coarse-cut, cooked cabbage, scented with carraway and juniper berries.

For main courses, the stuffed squab salutes the Haeberlin brothers, those three-starred chefs of Alsace. The sprightly seasoned stuffing is flawless and its slightly pungent bed of cabbage reminds us that Alsace borders upon sauerkraut-relishing Germany. Or if you cannot get enough of our California artichokes, try the medallions of veal Murat, fork-tender veal adorned with sliced artichoke bottoms. Yet, the lamb is unbeatable. The choice is dazzling and it's yours!

If you wish a light dessert after such an abundance of riches, their custards and Bavarian creams, festive with all manner of fresh fruits and berries, provide just the right light touch as a finale.

The wine list at Le Castel shows as much understanding as the menu. For example, on one evening I uncovered a superb champagne seldom encountered on menus: Billecart-Salmon. And while it might be no longer available, ask Mr. Frankel for his suggestions on other wines to enhance your dinner.

For even though its subdued atmosphere, correct service and exciting menu has made Le Castel the favored dining spot for a large segment San Francisco's most serious diners, Mr. Frankel is the consummate host and will graciously take the time to assist anyone who wishes his input in constructing a perfect dinner. Indeed, should you take my and his recommendations, you might come away saying that with Le Castel I have indeed saved the very best for the last.

10:30 p.m. The time has come to say good-bye or at least *au revoir, auf Wiedersehen, arrivederci*—so long. If you are remaining for a longer period than a week, the balance of this book will help you enjoy this extra time. But if you have to catch that next plane home, let me say I hope you have enjoyed our One Perfect Week in San Francisco together. I know I have enjoyed bringing it to you.

PART TWO

Two-, Three- and Four-Day Trips

Around San Francisco

A Two- or Three-Day Trip Up the
Coast to Mendocino

O.K. I admit it—I am in love with San Francisco. I have spent a great deal of time in nearly every nook and cranny of Europe, circled the Pacific, been just about everywhere. But San Francisco remains my favorite area in the world in which to live.

Why? Well, the pace is less hectic than in most major American metropolitan areas, yet there is an extraordinary variety of arts and entertainment, equal on a per capita basis to any great cultural center. The city's range of exciting dining places is a restaurant-goer's dream come true. Its weather is politely moderate, but should February's wetness get you down, you can always hop an hour's flight to Palm Springs to bask in the sun or drive only a few hours to the finest ski slopes in the West.

Perhaps most important is that San Francisco doesn't close you in. Its constant around-the-corner views, the consciousness of sky, the briskness of ocean breezes all alleviate the stifling asphalt-jungle aura of New York, or Tokyo, or Milan. And should you desire an even greater respite from steel and concrete, all you need do is drive but a few miles to find yourself in beautiful, unspoiled country, where pine needles crackle underfoot, the surf pounds and the stars are touchable. And this is exactly what we are going to share on our special side trip up the coast to Mendocino.

Almost all guidebooks to the San Francisco area place a visit to Carmel at the top of their "out-of-town" trips. And perhaps I would have done so, many, many years ago. But today, Carmel is primarily a shopping mecca for legions of visitors who clog the narrow streets endlessly circling the town's few square blocks in search of that nonexistent parking place.

So while I do recommend a visit to Carmel later on, tying it in with a journey down the Big Sur Coast to the Hearst Castle, I believe the ideal change of pace from city life to the open spaces is achieved by heading north to Mendocino.

First, we had better decide what to take along. Let's see. You will need only informal wear. The one restaurant which insists upon neckties, I boycott. So take some casual sunny weather togs (it never gets scorching hot, but it can be warm), as well as some sturdier stuff just in case the fog is in.

Also there is a nine-hole golf course at the Little River Inn, which is open to the public, as well as a Mendocino Tennis Club (for reservations: 707-937-0007). So throw in the appropriate sports gear.

But most important to me, the area claims some fine state parks with miles of hiking trails. So if you are into that—as I am—take along your hiking shoes. Should fishing be your hobby, steelhead and salmon abound here. Nightlife is absent from this rural scene so bring along your dominoes, cards and some good books. . . or just your desire for quiet. Oh yes, you will also need travelers checks or cash. Many of the restaurants and even hotels do not accept plastic.

And, of course, you'll need reservations.

Years ago, the Mendocino Coast around Little River was strictly a haven for fishermen. All they wanted ashore were a decent bed, a well-stocked bar, and wholesome no-nonsense grub. Then this incredibly beautiful coastline was "discovered" by vacationers and soon, the small town of Mendocino began to court artsy galleries, "shoppes" with cute names, and even a few of the inevitable tour buses.

But up to a few years ago, except perhaps on major summer weekends, you could simply pick up the phone and call your favorite hotel to be assured a room would be awaiting you that night. But last-minute reservations in almost any California resort area have become a thing of the past. So I suggest you reserve accommodations at one of my two recommended hotels as far in advance as possible.

My favorite spot up here for over thirty years has been the Little River Inn, Highway 1, Little River (three miles south of the town of Mendocino), (707) 937-5942. The inn proper, a white Maine-style building dating from 1853, stands on a small rise to the right of the highway, looking out over an inlet and the endless Pacific. From its front porch, pioneers once stood watch for arriving sailing vessels which brought long-awaited news from the East and fresh provisions. You now can stand there and spot a salmon fleet or perhaps even some migrating gray whales.

Over the years its once Spartan rooms have been upgraded into homey but attractive and comfortable accommodations. And my favorite rooms not only have marine views but working fireplaces. A few years ago, the Little River Inn also added tennis courts for its guests, but you will find no phone or TV set in your room. For which I am grateful. When I come up to Mendocino, I want to get away from it all. And I mean *all*!

Getting away from it all is what this whole trip is about. With its neighbor-friendly staff and picturesque white-picket-fence setting—on returning to your room after dinner, you will often find wild deer grazing on the lawn—the Little River Inn is the ideal get-away spot.

Another far newer place to stay is Hill House, 10701 Palette Drive, Mendocino, (707) 937-0554. Its greatest advantage is that it is located right on the edge of the charming town of Mendocino. Hill House also has some rooms and suites overlooking the Pacific, but many rooms have no views at all. The decor is sort of kitschy Victorian and rooms have the modern "conveniences" of direct-dail phones and TVs.

If you fail to get into either of these two places, here are two phone numbers you can use to find alternatives. A call to (707) 964-3153 puts you in touch with the Mendocino Coast Chamber of Commerce, who can often tell you which hotels have vacancies. Or with a call to Mendocino Coast Reservations, (800) 262-7801, you might be able to arrange a rental at either a private home available for vacationers or at one of the many bed and breakfasts in the area.

THE FIRST DAY

Whenever and wherever I travel, I like to get started early. I prefer early morning departures, be it by train, plane, bus or car. It seems to me that if I plan to leave later in the day, I just fritter away the morning hours waiting to go and rechecking to see if I have packed everything. But today your departure time is actually more dependent upon which route you elect to take.

If I can recommend two places to stay on the Mendocino Coast, I can recommend three routes to get you there.

The first is the longest in terms of time—over five hours—but is one of the most spectacular routes in California. It follows Highway 1 all along the coast. However, it has some drawbacks.

First of all, much of this route is pretty rough driving—mile upon mile of hairpin turns on a narrow road carved out of mountainsides that fall off to the surf below. Secondly, I have never found anyplace memorable at which to lunch along the way. And thirdly, my favorite place to lunch in Mendocino closes at 2:30 p.m.; therefore, reaching it on time is chancy even with a fairly early departure.

The other two routes are faster and while not as totally spectacular they are both quite beautiful. Another important consideration is that they pass right by John Ash & Company, a restaurant (closed Monday; no lunch on Saturday; brunch on Sundays) which presents superb California cuisine in a lovely setting right on the edge of a vineyard.

Knowing those facts, the decision is yours. If you decide on the longer, more scenic route, I suggest a hearty pre-departure breakfast; if you take either of the other two easier routes, have a light breakfast since in less than two hours you will be at John Ash, which by the way also stops serving lunch at 2 p.m.

So, with the car packed, head out to now familiar Van Ness Avenue, turn left onto Lombard Street and cross the Golden Gate Bridge.

About four miles north of the bridge, you will see a sign indicating "Mill Valley, Stinson Beach, Highway 1." This is the dividing point of the routes. If you have decided on the longest and most spectacular route, take this turnoff to the right; if you are taking either of the other shorter ways, stay on the freeway heading north.

For a few pages, let me accompany those taking the long Highway 1 route. Even if you are not going this way, you might want to find out what you are missing.

You will remember the first few miles of Highway 1, if you took the Muir Woods outing recommended on the Third Day's schedule. However, Highway 1 soon becomes filled with twists and turns as it roller-coasters over the headlands to the ocean. From their crests on a clear day, you can see forever. . . and that includes portions of San Francisco even though you are now in the country.

After dipping to sea level at Muir Beach, Highway 1 shoots abruptly upward again and suddenly below you are the sands of Stinson Beach.

The next stretch is along gentle cattle-grazing land and through sleepy little hamlets like Olema and Marshall. Along Tomales Bay you will see oyster farms, but unfortunately, these oysters are enormous and not particularly appealing, at least to me.

Highway 1 now cuts inland through more dairy land and through Bodega Bay. In this little town, known for its salmon fleet, Alfred Hitchcock shot his classic "The Birds." Remember when Tippi Hedren was suddenly attacked by that first gull? Well, it was right in the middle of that small harbor on your left.

By the way, if you got away late and will not be able to reach Mendocino (still some 3 hours away) in time for the 2:30 p.m. lunch curfew, you might lunch here at The Tides. The only dish I have enjoyed here is the salmon, but then salmon is *the* fish along this entire route and you will be savoring it superbly prepared at the Little River Inn, so I do hope you love salmon!

Ten miles further at Jenner, Highway 1 crosses a high bridge spanning the mouth of the Russian River. (Those taking my second recommended route will travel the rest of this route, having arrived at Jenner from inland.)

Thirteen miles of some incredible cliffside driving brings you in sight of Fort Ross. Not too long ago, Highway 1 ran right through this old wooden fort but, in order to better preserve the historic spot, the highway now skirts the high stockade. If you wish to visit the fort, you must park in a lot to the left of Highway 1 and take a long walk. This is a great place for a welcomed leg-stretch.

Fort Ross was constructed in 1812, when a party of Russians accompanied by native Alaskans landed here. Their purpose in erecting the fort was multiple: to plant wheat for their Alaskan settlements, to hunt for otter, and to trade with the Spaniards who owned California but had advanced only as far north as San Francisco. In fact, the Spaniards never knew about Fort Ross until it was too late. And as you can see, the fort's strategic position enabled the Russians to decline all "invitations" to leave. Only a couple of buildings still stand and even they have been restored. In the northeast corner is a chapel, while in the southeast is an octagonal blockhouse with gun emplacements facing the sea, the primary access to the fort until the 1920's.

After leaving Fort Ross, continue on up Highway 1 and watch for The Timber Cove Lodge on the left. This is a charming place to stay, if you wish a shorter trip. Almost every room has an oceanview and a hot tub. And that fantastic totem is by Benny Bufano, the famed San Francisco sculptor of the Sun Yat Sen statue in St. Mary's Square and whose madonna figure greets you at the airport.

Seventy-five miles after Fort Ross, you will find yourself in the Mendocino area—our destination.

Now then, for those traveling either of the two faster routes up Highway 101, the road is almost arrow-straight, through Marin County's bedroom communities.

After Santa Rosa, watch for the "Russian River/ Guerneville" turnoff on the right (about 55 miles from the Golden Gate Bridge Toll Plaza).

Take this turnoff, then turn left onto River Road, which spans the freeway. Take the first left on the west side of the freeway onto Barnes Road and then another left into the Vintners Inn parking area. You have arrived at John Ash & Company, 4330 Barnes Rd. off River Rd., Santa Rosa, (707) 527-7687 (reservations recommended). I cannot think of a more ideal setting in which to experience California cuisine than in this beautiful adobe-colored, stuccoed restaurant.

If you wish to dine indoors, you will be seated in spacious rooms with vaulted ceilings done in a smart cream and light burgundy color scheme. However, weather permitting, I prefer the flower-bedecked outdoor dining terrace overlooking the vineyards.

The menu changes constantly, since Mr. Ash is a freshness fanatic. Evidently he has scoured the area to uncover the finest in field-fresh vegetables. As for the herbs that perfume his creations, they are picked right from the little garden off the terrace.

He then combines these impeccable ingredients into classic dishes which shine with individual touches, often giving evidence of his fascination with both the beauty and delicacy of Japanese cookery.

For example, his onion soup "Les Halles" is not the carmelized thick version, but rather an almost clear stock, heavenly scented with fresh herbs and filled with slices of translucent onions. The topping is a bubbly crust of jack and gruyere cheese, gratineed to perfection.

There is also a photogenic plate of gravlax—glorious, tissue-thin slices of that preserved salmon, garnished with a dollop of caviar and fresh basil sprigs.

For main courses, a flank steak—marinated in garlic, chilies and herbs—will be grilled precisely to your specifications and sliced. You can then place the beef upon perfect warm tortillas, adding black bean salsa and grilled red onions to create the ultimate fajita. Or the breast of chicken will be far more moist—a characteristic almost impossible to encounter in restaurants!—than elsewhere. And the bed of steamed oriental greens, aromatic in their soy-ginger vinaigrette, provides a vivacious flavor constrast.

Desserts often feature the fruits and berries for which this area—Luther Burbank country—is justly famed. For example, the fresh summer fruit cobbler, served warm with a scoop of vanilla ice cream, can feature such exotica as yellow raspberries.

The wine list is impressive. And luckily, because you are doing a lot of driving and perhaps do not wish a full bottle, many fine Sonoma wines are available by the glass. And that includes one of my favorite Chardonnays—Sonoma Cutrer. All in all, unquestionably one of the finest country restaurants in the West.

Even if you chose not to lunch at John Ash, this juncture is the dividing spot between the two remaining routes to Mendocino. You now can either head directly to the coast (some 28 miles away), or continue further on Highway 101, turning toward the coast some 29 miles later, immediately after the town of Cloverdale. If you head directly for the coast, the trip to Mendocino will take about three hours more. If you return to 101 and then head to the coast later, the trip will take about two more hours.

I prefer to head for the coast now, by leaving the John Ash parking area to the right, then left on River Road, so named because it basically follows the Russian River. River Road winds through redwood forests and funky little vacation towns like Forestville, where you cross the river, and Guerneville.

Guerneville, once a popular resort area, had gone into a decline in the 60s. Then, at the height of the gay liberation movement, it became a swinging gay summer resort, rivaling New York's Fire Island. However, with the advent of AIDS that era passed, too. And now it's back to being a rather quiet, slightly seedy, rustic little town.

At Guerneville you join Highway 116, by-passing Monte Rio. At the junction with Highway 1, head north, following the signs to Jenner and Fort Bragg. (For a description of the route from here to Mendocino, see the first recommended route, earlier in this chapter.)

If you opt for my third suggested route, return to Highway 101 and head north. This is a very pleasant drive, passing through gently rolling hills and areas of vineyards. Right past Cloverdale (about 84 miles from San Francisco) take a turnoff to the left marked "Highway 128 Boonville." And in about 28 miles you will find yourself in the small town of Boonville.

Actually, this is quite an interesting town in one unusual respect—it has its own language. There is a totally foreign Boonville vocabulary, the origins of which are unknown. For example, above a pay phone on the main street you will find the words "Bucky Waller." That's their name for a telephone. Why? Locals are unsure, but many think that the first phone in town was owned by one Bucky Waller and thus that new-fangled invention was named after its first owner. And if you want a cup of coffee, that's a "horn of zeese."

But if you did not stop at John Ash & Co for lunch, you might be interested in more than coffee. And the place to go is the Boonville Hotel, on the left side of Highway 128, Boonville, (707) 895-3478. (Its days open vary with the time of year, so it's best to call in advance. *No credit cards*.)

If you have read the previous edition of this guide, please understand that this is *not* the famed restaurant that once occupied this location and was regarded as one of the finest in the West. That Mecca for gourmets suddenly and inexplicably did not open for business one morning or ever again. Its owners had quietly left town—and country—for France.

But even with an extremely limited menu of light luncheon fare, the current Boonville Hotel can be just as exciting as its highfalutin predecessor. Seldom have I enjoyed a lunch where I sampled over 80% of the offerings and could not find a single fault in any of the diverse dishes! And each had enormous individuality and excitement.

A mixed green salad with vinaigrette was composed of

the variety and quality that usually reduces East Coast visitors to tears. And the perfectly modulated dressing did just that—dressed the greens not smothered them.

A quesadilla of cabbage, jack cheese and scallions in mole sauce, puzzled me when I saw it on the menu. But I was instantly won over by the perfect tortillas, holding molten jack cheese and threads of sliced cabbage, that lightened what could be a heavy filling. And parading along the top of the quesadilla were a seemingly minutes-old green salsa, a warmly chilied mole sauce, plus the perfect black beans.

Ever heard of a restaurant that can produce a scintillating Mexican dish like quesadilla and also come up with pizza with pizzazz? Well, now you have. I have sampled all kinds of pizzas in my life, including those simple but lusty ones in Naples. This pizza's dough was more refined—almost buttery. It was also outlandishly flavorful. And the topping? A fresh tomato sauce, melted cheese, squares of pepper bacon and infinitely sweet glazed onion, all set off with garden-fresh rosemary. Marinated onions highlighted a seared but succulent chicken breast, served with a tantalizing chutney, all on a bed of arugula.

Whoever does the baking the Boonville is a champion, whether it is pizzas, quesadillas or bread (do not miss their special homemade bread). And he or she also knows the art of fine pastries as well. Because the chocolate layer cake was the quintessential triple-layer beauty that I thought existed only in my fondest childhood memories. This was a far lighter creation—but in no way light on chocolate flavor!—than the current rage in chocolate cakes which approach candy-bar consistency.

But then I might be made to forgo this masterpiece, for a warm-from-the-oven biscuit, covered with a strawberry-rhubarb mixture and served with a creme anglaise instead of whipped cream. The ultimate shortcake!

And this culinary finesse will not bankrupt you. None of these luncheon dishes costs more than $10. Plus there is an intriguing variety of local wines—Navarro, Handley, Lazy Creek, Husch—by the glass. It's a great way to do a little wine tasting with your lunch. By the way, almost all of these wineries are located along Highway 128, as it takes you through beautiful Anderson Valley to the coast.

If you are not planning to return to San Francisco via this route, you might consider making a stop at some of the wineries for further sampling and perhaps purchase. Many, like Navarro, are almost impossible to find in liquor stores.

Also, at the far end of the valley, you will find the Roederer Vineyards (open by appointment only). This is where yet another famed French vintner has taken advantage of California's superb wine-producing potential. Naturally, Roederer would never call their sparkling wine "champagne," but it's awfully good.

On leaving the Anderson Valley, Highway 128 takes you through a breathtaking redwood forest where you drive down avenues of the giants. Then on to the Pacific Ocean, some thirty miles after Boonville. When you meet up with Highway 1, head north.

Now then, if for any reason you have not had lunch regardless of the route you chose, I hope for your sake it is not 2:30 p.m. yet. Because that is when the Cafe Beaujolais, my favorite luncheon spot in the area, closes.

So if it is nearing that time, continue on through the tiny town of Little River, even if you are staying at the Little River Inn—which you will see on your right—to the town of Mendocino.

Turn left at the "Business District" sign into the town proper. Then turn right off Main Street onto Howard for one block, then right onto Ukiah to number 961, and dash into the unassuming little house that is the Cafe Beaujolais, Mendocino, (707) 937-5614, (open daily for breakfast and lunch; and for dinners on weekend nights in season; *no credit cards*).

Actually, if the afternoon is sunny, you might wish to lunch on a glass-walled outdoor dining area in the back, overlooking a charming rose-filled garden and with a view of the coastline.

I honestly doubt whether a canned or frozen vegetable—God forbid, a preservative!—has ever found its way into this bastion of freshness and culinary honesty. Just catch your breath while you bask in the luxuriant natural sweetness of a truly fresh cream of broccoli soup. Their clam chowder is not the unctuously thick porridge most San Francisco restaurants serve, but a true milky chowder, filled with clams, new potatoes, bacon and celery.

For a main course, Beaujolais' Mendocino fish stew is gloriously fresh rock fish sauteed with white wine, flavored with tomatoes, olives and basil, and spiked with hot peppers. This winning creation is served over brown rice. For something deliciously offbeat, the black bean chili is the ultimate vegetarian bean dish, enlivened with cumin, coriander, and cheese, but pacified by sour cream. And I hope there are three in your party, because the Chinese chicken salad should not be missed. The chicken breast, marinated in sherry, soy sauce and five-spice seasoning, is baked and then thinly sliced. Tossed with lettuce and crisp rice noodles, it is then dressed with a sesame oil vinaigrette. Sensational!

For dessert, Beaujolais usually whips up one of those diet-defying chocolate things, such as a ground nut-textured, sensuous Queen Mother's Torte. Or an equally lethal buttercream caramel bar sundae—a warm, chewy oatmeal-nut cookie, oozing with caramel, topped with vanilla ice cream, chocolate fudge sauce and toasted nuts. And if you like the true tang of fresh lemons in a dessert, the lemon curd tart, with a bewitchingly buttery crust, is for you.

Naturally, all desserts, as well as all the superb breads, are baked on the premises.

By the way, if the Beaujolais serves superb lunches, it is even more famous for its breakfasts. And it would be criminal for you to miss the opportunity to relish dishes such as their waffle of buttermilk, cornmeal and oatmeal. You can have it served with real, honest-to-God maple syrup, not that liquid sugar, imitation stuff! Or you might like to try their brioche bread French toast.

Your orange or grapefruit juice will be squeezed to order.

The bacon is fresh off the skillet and sausages can be deliciously unusual, such as chicken-apple. Still hungry? The coffee cake is unbeatable. The moca latte, a delicious blending of hot chocolate, espresso and steamed milk is my favorite breakfast beverage in the world! So schedule a breakfast visit to Cafe Beaujolais sometime during your stay.

After a final sip of some of Beaujolais' peerless coffee, it is time to drive to your hotel. That means, if you are staying at the Little River Inn, simply retrace your route back down Highway 1.

If you are staying at Hill House, on leaving the Cafe Beaujolais, turn left to Lansing Street, right on Lansing until you see the Hill House sign on Palette Drive on the right.

There is no need for me to plan the remainder of your afternoon. You will want to unpack and rest up after that long drive. If it is sunny, and you are at the Little River Inn, you might wish to walk down to the beach at Van Damme State Park adjacent to the inn. Or if you are at Hill House, a stroll through Mendocino might be nice. Otherwise, just collapse in front of your view of the ocean and relax.

For dinner, there are two different places I can recommend—the Little River Inn, and the Little River Restaurant which is located right across Highway 1 from the Little River Inn driveway.

The Little River Restaurant, Highway 1, Little River, (707) 937-4945, (dinners only; check for days open; reservations a must; *no credit cards*), is probably one of the coziest and smallest restaurants I have ever come across. Its seating capacity peaks at 16 and I would not accept the table in the door on a blustery night. The uni-sex toilet is outside around the corner—its key hangs by the wine cabinet inside the front door. The kitchen is so small that Ms. Barrett, the owner-chef who does all the cooking personally, must move away from the stove when the refrigerator door is opened. This kind of closet-close quarters requires that they adhere to a strict two-seating policy—6 and 8:30. And if the service seems slow, it is only because it is measured to the pace of the kitchen.

On my last visit, Ms. Barrett was still slowly transforming the repertory inherited from the previous chef into her own. But even if things change, I don't think you will be disappointed by her nice sense of balance and flavors.

For example, a mushroom-basil soup was totally delicious: piping hot, with the minced fresh mushrooms still retaining enough size to impart texture as well as flavor. A tiny sour cream float and a sprinkle of cayenne capped it nicely.

Then came a lovely salad of fresh greens, shaved carrot and cabbage all smartly attired in balsamic vinegar dressing.

As for main courses, the rack of lamb was fine—cooked to my desired degree of underdoneness—but I thought the apple-brandy-garlic sauce was a little contradictory to the lamb's basic flavor. However, the ginger-scallion sauce on the absolutely tender slices of roast pork was ideal. Both dishes were accompanied by a melange of totally fresh vegetables and some ideally steamed new potatoes.

Desserts—a beautifully old-fashioned white cake with a Cointreaux-enhanced frosting and a gelato-dense chocolate truffle ice cream—were top drawer. And when you consider these complete dinners were available for around $20 each, then you have a delightful, cozy find on the Mendocino Coast.

THE SECOND DAY

Since these few days on the Mendocino Coast should be free of all pressures and big-city regimens, you will not find me putting together an hour-by-hour activity schedule for you. Just do your own thing. But if you don't mind, I will join you for breakfast, an irresistible meal at Little River Inn.

You can start with a brimming glass of freshly-squeezed orange juice. Yes, it's not "reconstituted from concentrate" or any of that ersatz orange stuff astronauts supposedly thrive on. This usually sets my palate up for a big plate of the Inn's Swedish hot cakes, piping hot, paper-thin and delectably light, accompanied by a few strips of crisp thick-cut bacon. Eggs are done any way you want them. There is plenty of toast, but I cannot resist the freshly baked muffins.

Anyhow, with this stick-to-your-ribs lumberjack breakfast under your belt, some type of exercise is called for. So how about heading to the golf course or tennis courts or going for a nice long hike? And with Van Damme Park right next door and Russian Gulch State Park and Jughandle State Reserve just a few miles up Highway 1, you have some great options.

If you select Van Damme Park and its Fern Canyon you can start out on your hike without moving your car or even setting foot on the highway. For right from the Inn's driveway, there is a trail that takes you above Highway 1 and directly to the park's entrance. Here you turn right and head into the park.

In minutes you are past the campers and tents and heading into a narrow, shady canyon, its walls covered with literally millions of ferns as well as towering redwoods and Douglas fir. And depending on the time of the year, you will also see a vast variety of blooming plants, including trillium, calypso orchids, and rhododendron.

The hike in through Fern Canyon is an easy one. However, if you wish to visit the Pygmy Forest, you will have to take a steeper trail up to the crest.

And a Pygmy Forest—either here or at Jughandle—should not be missed. Here just about every tree which grows in the area can be seen in miniature form. Due to a lack of nutrients in the soil, fully matured firs and pines reach a height of only a few feet. It's an intriguing sight. (If you cannot make the trek on foot, you can reach the Pygmy Forest by car. Just take the Little River Airport Road, which hits Highway 1 just south of Little River, and drive about three and a half miles inland.)

Another nearby park, Russian Gulch Park, offers more fine hikes—one of a similar nature which ends at a lovely waterfall, and another which takes you out onto the windswept headlands. In addition, Russian Gulch Park provides a picnic area with a dramatic view of the ocean and the entrance to the gulch.

If you decide to enjoy Russian Gulch Park, you might wish to pick up those picnic provisions at the Main Street Delicatessen in Mendocino—it's right on your way. All you need do is head north up Highway 1 from the Little River Inn. Along Highway 1, you will pass grazing fields and old, tumble-down barns seemingly in wait for Andrew Wyeth to come by and capture on canvas the last of their kind.

In about three miles, turn left into the town of Mendocino, swinging right onto Main Street. On one side is a bluff overlooking Mendocino Bay, while on the other are shops and a hotel dating from 1878. But more about that later. Right now we need to find the Main Street Delicatessen at number 45040 and pick up some provisions. This might include a bottle of local wine. A Handley chardonnay or a Navarro gewurztraminer would do nicely.

With our mission completed, head back out of Mendocino the way you entered. But at the intersection with Highway 1, turn left and proceed a few miles north to Russian Gulch (turnoff on left of highway). Right after passing the park entrance, where you will pay a small day-use fee, continue on ahead. Immediately on the right, take note of a turnoff, which would take you to the picnic area. But for now proceed straight ahead and soon you will pass under the bridge that arches high over the canyon's mouth. Drive through the camp to the furthest parking area. As you approach, on the right you will spot a trail sign indicating "South Trail."

When you park, you can decide which hike you wish to take. If you proceed straight ahead from the parking area, you will find a trail very similar to that at Van Damme Park. This one also follows a stream deep into a huge, fern-covered canyon. The reward at the end of a short but somewhat steep climb is lovely, 36-foot high Russian Gulch Falls. Your other choice is to visit the spectacular Mendocino headlands.

To reach them, walk back to that "South Trail" marker

and take that trail. It will first lead you up the south side of the canyon, then under the Highway 1 bridge and out onto the headlands. Here you will find yourself on a wildflower-covered, wind-swept bluff with the foam-spewing, crashing waves of the Pacific pounding below you. It is an awesome spot. And if you look across the canyon to the headlands on the north side, you will be able to spot your luncheon picnic area.

When you have had enough of the majesty of the ocean's might, simply retrace your steps to your car, then drive back up the same road by which you arrived. Before you reach the park exit, turn left into the picnic area for lunch. Even the most mundane ham sandwich tastes ambrosial to me when consumed on this spot after a nice long hike!

After lunch, you might enjoy a walk out onto this headland, but watch out for the poison oak! Here you can see the Devil's Punch Bowl, a sea-cut tunnel 200 hundred feet in length which has collapsed at its inland end to produce a hole 100 feet in diameter and 60 feet deep. However, the waves pushing through the tunnel only create the "blowhole" effect during heavy storms, which I hope is not the weather condition today!

A third nearby park, Jughandle State Reserve, is further north up Highway 1. (Be sure to take along two quarters in order to purchase a map of the area, which includes pertinent information on the Ecological Staircase, from a dispensing machine at the reserve's parking area on the left of Highway 1).

I cannot recommend Jughandle too highly, especially if you have school-aged children along or if you have an interest in how the forces of nature sculpted this area.

For at Jughandle, you can walk the Ecological Staircase, a totally fascinating, self-guided nature trail. Although it will take you about three hours to cover its five rather easy miles, it will take you back in time some half million years.

As you walk along the well-marked trail, you will find some 30 sign posts. And with your map-guide, you will be able to read about the significance of each particular spot.

And apart from the intriguing educational aspect, the walker is also rewarded with rare beauty—massive redwoods, pines and wildflowers. And at the top, a pygmy forest. Truly not to be missed.

After any one of these hikes, you may wish to explore the village of Mendocino at greater length. (I assume you were not tempted by the shops, when you picked up your lunch at the deli.) So find your way back to Mendocino from whichever park you are in. That should be easy enough, since Highway 1 is the only road connecting everything in the area!

I love Mendocino as a town. Even though T-shirt shops—those unwelcome harbingers of mass tourism—are cropping up, there are still some excellent galleries featuring local art and handicrafts. And then there is always that unbeatable location with the Pacific Ocean across Main Street.

There are two stops you should not miss.

The first is the Mendocino Hotel at 45080 Main Street. Be sure to drop into this 100-year-old establishment, superbly restored to its Victorian elegance.

Another compulsory stop for me is the last building north on Main Street. Here in the tiny Marilyn Douglas Mendocino Jams & Jellies shop you can purchase some of the finest preserves you have ever tasted. If you took any of the hikes, you surely must have noticed the vast quantities of berries which grow in this area. Well, Marilyn Douglas preserves them without the use of any extenders or preservatives. Her wild blackberry and her boysenberry are incomparable! Often, there are a few flavors to taste, so you can verify my high estimation on the spot. She will also ship her products anywhere in the U.S.A.

When you have had enough walking about, I am sure I need not convince you just how soothing it would be to return to your hotel and laze in a chair overlooking the bay, and take in the sea and the high sky filled with white clouds. At times I have done just that and, perhaps with the distraction of a good book, soon found myself lightyears removed from San Francisco and routine.

Another wonderful thing for me about this area is the fact that you don't have to dress for dinner. And tonight, you don't even have to change out of your hiking wear to dine at the dining room of the Little River Inn.

Over the years I have been coming to the Inn, the kitchen and dining room have undergone a number of changes, even being an outside concession at one time. And as I write this, the kitchen in now under the control of a new young chef, who seems to be having a very good influence on the cuisine.

For example, a recent lentil soup was totally delicious. Not the thick type in which you could stand a spoon, but a light stock filled with the flavor of lentils, studded with large pieces of onion and carrot. And the salad of impeccable garden-fresh greens lost its former inexplicable topping of frozen green peas. Hurray!

With the salmon fleet in view off the front porch, you can be assured that this fish will be fresh. And the Little River's kitchen understands that the preservation of the salmon's sweet moistness is achieved by judicious cooking. Therefore, your salmon will be dusted with a film of cracker crumbs and sauteed just long enough to cook it through, but not to dehydrate it.

For years, the Little River Inn was *the* place in the West for abalone. In fact, it used to appear on even the breakfast menu! But with the near extinction of that delectable snail (yes, that's what an abalone is actually!), it vanished from the menu. However, recently the abalone has made sporadic reappearances on the dinner menu. When you order it, your waitress will ask that you tell them immediately if it is tough. Escoffier himself could not soften a tough abalone. And they can, at times, be tough and rubbery. But if they are not, they are a heavenly dish. On the other hand, for those who prefer meat, there is quite a respectable New York steak.

One aspect of the inn's cooking that has changed, and for the better, is their vegetables. At one time, all you could hope for was canned corn. Now, I have encountered a smooth squash puree on one evening and Chinese-crisp green vegetables on another. But I have also encountered abused rice.

For dessert, one of my favorites on this planet—a down-home, piping hot ollieberry cobbler that tantalizes your taste buds with an ideally slight undersweetness. And while it is usually served with ice cream, I prefer a topping of real whipped-cream. Coffee would only keep me up, even after an active day like this!

THE THIRD DAY

This day could just as easily be the fourth or the fifth, depending upon how much time you want to spend in this wonderful area. But eventually, it will be time to start back to San Francisco. And if today is the day for your return, I have some suggestions.

To return, you can simply drive back on one of the three routes I recommended for your journey north. For example, if you missed lunch at either John Ash or The Boonville, you might want to take a route that will allow you to lunch or dine there.

Or. . . if you wish for a longer stay in this wonderful area of California, and if you have read ahead to make the necessary reservations, you could continue your Northern California tour by now heading to the Benbow Inn, 445 Lake Benbow Drive, (707) 923-2124.

Here in the midst of the mighty redwoods stands this National Historical Landmark, which has played host to international figures and localites alike since 1926. Recently restored, the Benbow welcomes you with graciousness, charm and such niceties as English tea with scones in the afternoon.

During the day you can play tennis, take horseback rides, golf on the nine-hole course, swim in Benbow Lake or hike through the magnificent redwood forests. In the evening, a surprisingly fine restaurant welcomes you. The Benbow is a cherished getaway for scores of Bay Area residents, so reservations should be made as far in advance as possible.

To reach the Benbow, head north on Highway 1 through Fort Bragg and then through Westport and Rockport and on to Leggett. At Leggett you join up with Highway 101, taking it for approximately 21 miles to the Benbow Inn. (Total distance from Mendocino to the Benbow Inn is about 78 miles.) After your stay at the Benbow, you simply take Highway 101 right back to San Francisco.

Well, back in San Francisco, what's for dinner? Maybe after jeans and hiking boots for a couple of days, a tie or fashionable frock might be a nice change. And that's just what the subdued but elegant atmosphere of my favorite up-scale Italian restaurant calls for.

Acquerello, 1722 Sacramento Street (between Polk and Van Ness; 567-5432; open Tuesday through Saturday for dinner only; reservations imperative), is a stylish, small restaurant—all white and refined. But the plates which emerge from the kitchen positively sing.

The melodies are not the robust *canzone* of a Neapolitan fisherman, but rather cultivated art songs which capitivate you with their shadings and subtleties. This is a fine *ristorante* not a *trattoria*.

As you look over the limited but extremely well conceived menu, the maitre d' will pour you a complimentary glass of an Italian sparkling wine—a spumante. And then it's decisions, decisions.

The mussels Lucese-style are some of the finest I have encountered. And while garlic is in the liquid in which they have been steamed, it is not flagrantly used. And, by the way, I would not hesitate for a moment in sopping up that delicious essence with some of the fine bread. But if you opt for the mussels, you will miss out on the ultimate carpaccio—not of beef but veal, drizzled with a provocative lemon-egg sauce. All too often the seemingly raw, razor-thin meat in a carpaccio is stunned by a storm of capers, cheese, etc. But not here. Then there is always some kind of salad on hand; the menu changes regularly. Here again, the kitchen shows infinite finesse in wedding, for example, the tenderest of spinach leaves and pear slices with shavings of parmesan and a sprinkling of sesame seeds.

If you think choosing from those antipasti is difficult, your problems have just begun as you hit the pasta section. I have enjoyed about seven different pastas here and none was less than superb! For example, the kitchen creates cloud-light little Italian dumplings (gnocchetti) and whether they are of spinach with a sweet gorgonzola sauce or of pumpkin with black truffles and sage, they are incredible!

The maccheroni in the chitarra style was delicious—and made me laugh to recall those limp dishes I had in the Abruzzi, where chitarra originates. The bewitching sauce was of roasted peppers with pieces of capon. The penne with a highly aromatic rosemary sauce (also slightly creamy) was thickened with shreds of rabbit. And while I found a special ravioli almost too adventuresome on paper—a venison stuffing and a port wine sauce filled with pomegranate seeds!—its realization was exciting and delicious.

When it comes to main courses, Acquerello avoids the "Italian Syndrome"—main dishes that are a letdown after soaring pastas—better than any Italian restaurant in town. Although I did find the lamb chops sliced awfully thin, they were nicely tender and basked happily in extra virgin olive oil, flavored with herbs and juniper berries. In the top-marks category was a stellar filet of beef rolled around a filling of chard, sausage and fennel in a rich tomato-wine sauce. Competing with it were custardy sweetbreads in a simple wild mushroom sauce. Accompanying vegetables can be intriguing—a purposely tepid, slightly sweet eggplant melange or julienned fennel, for example.

For dessert, Acquerello comes up with some traditional Italian beauties—housemade ice creams and sherbets, a stunning creamy flan, and a deliciously simple, moist Italian apple cake. Add to this a wine list which promotes some of Italy's finest, along with considerate service without the unnerving intensity of many Italian dining rooms, and you have a truly elegant dining experience in both ambience and cuisine.

Acquerello is located on Sacramento Street between

Polk and Van Ness, with validated parking across the street.

Now then, for those of you who don't want to change out of your driving clothes and are looking for a more casual light meal before returning to your hotel, I recommend Tommaso's, 1042 Kearny Street off Broadway, (398-9696; open nightly except Monday; no reservations).

Located just a tassel's throw from North Beach's honky-tonk topless row, Tommaso's is also Italian but of the *con gusto* Neapolitan variety.

When you open the heavy front door, you will be greeted by the strong aroma—perfume to me—of an oak fire. And it is over its glowing coals, that Tommaso's bakes their pizzas—the best in town.

These are real authentic Italian pizze. Not that totally American cardboard stuff so readily available in drive-ins, dime stores and even movie theaters! Nor the new-wave, elegantized pizza, like the one you may have enjoyed at the Boonville Hotel.

Just take a look at the dough—it has a lovely full-bodied flavor all its own; its edges are light and fluffy. And the toppings available are classic.

However, often I by-pass a pizza and opt for Tommaso's glorious calzone. A calzone is made of the same ingredients as a pizza, but here the dough is not flat but rather folded over the mozzarella, ricotta, sausage, tomato sauce, and mushroom filling. It's an Italian turnover *par excellence*! If there are more than two in your party, I would certainly order one pizza and the calzone #14.

While you are waiting for your pizza to emerge bubbling hot from that oven, try some of Tommaso's great salads. Fresh broccoli, almost crisp string beans or sweet roasted green peppers are treated to vinegar or lemon-accented, simple dressings. And they are simply delicious.

For dessert, inquire if the canoli have been refrigerated for long. (By the way, the friendly family at Tommaso's never seems to mind such probing.) If the canoli are fresh, these crispy tubes stuffed with sweetened ricotta are sensational. However, if they have served time in the refrigerator, they can become soggy, losing their most endearing quality.

The coffee is suavely Neapolitan and an ideal way to end your evening's visit to bella Napoli. (Driving directly to Tommaso's from Mendocino, simply take Lombard Street from the Golden Gate Bridge; turn right on Van Ness; then left down Broadway to Kearny Street.)

A Four-Day Trip to Carmel,

Monterey, Big Sur and San Simeon

Certainly the most popular out-of-town side trip for any first-time San Francisco visitor is to Carmel some 130 miles to the south.

Carmel initially achieved its fame by being the epitome of the sleepy seaside hamlet, replete with a rather quaint artsy-craftsy character. And it still valiantly strives to maintain its village aura by eschewing streetlights and house numbers. Many of the houses are constructed in picturesque styles which smack of the kind of architecture usually reserved for illustrations in children's books. With this storyland ambience, it is easy to understand why a Carmel stay was once considered the ideal balm to soothe the psyche, traumatized by modern urban hurly-burly.

However, as word got around hordes of city dwellers the world over wanted to partake of the Carmel elixir and, in so doing, they changed many of the very qualities they sought. In their effort to escape big-city commercialism and pressure, they created a type of countrified commercialism.

Carmel has therefore evolved from the idyllic little village-by-the-sea, into a handsome shopper's mecca, complete with all the problems which come hand-in-hand with that kind of "success." And while you still won't find any neon signs or fast-food purveyors on Ocean Avenue, you will find the latest in international haute-couturier creations, costly antiques, and acres of art.

Because, as I mentioned earlier in this book, I am not enamored with shopping *per se*, Carmel in this role holds little interest for me.

But. . . Carmel happens to be situated in the heart of one of the most scenically spectacular parts of California, if not the entire United States. Its neighbor to the north, Monterey, is extremely interesting historically and contains some lovely buildings dating from the time when it was the state's capital. Monterey also boasts one of the finest aquariums in the nation.

Carmel's neighbor to the south is the awesome Big Sur Coast, possibly the most majestic meeting of sea and land in the world. And a little further south is The Hearst Castle, awesome in a totally different way. Therefore, lovely Carmel, with its bevy of smart shops and galleries, is a "must-see" especially when enjoyed as part of this unique experience.

THE FIRST DAY

Of course, because of the area's enormous popularity, the visitor to the Carmel area first and foremost needs a hotel reservation. And in the summer it may be hard to come by.

For years, the only place I recommended was the Tickle Pink. And it is still my favorite. However, because reservations here are often difficult to come by and its location (four miles south of Carmel in the Highlands) can cause some frustration in traffic jams, I will offer two other suggestions.

But first let me tell you about the Tickle Pink Country Inn, 155 Highlands Drive, Carmel, 93923, (408) 624-1244.

Actually, The Tickle Pink is an extremely comfortable, modern motor inn. But because it is perched on a cliffside overlooking the Pacific Ocean, just about every room—from the most modest to the lovely suites with hot tubs and wood-burning fireplaces—shares this view. And that gives it an important advantage over the vast majority of hotels and motels in Carmel proper. And almost every room has a balcony overlooking the sea, where you can savor your morning continental breakfast, presented with the compliments of the inn.

What has also made the Tickle Pink my favorite for over 30 years is the fact that it is located four miles south of Carmel. I still like its removal from the town, although today that can have its drawbacks when I find myself stuck in traffic trying to get into Carmel or Monterey for dinner. But the Tickle Pink is still tops for me.

If you wish to stay right in Carmel, then I would recommend the beautiful La Playa Hotel, Camino Real and 8th Avenue, Carmel, (within California call 408 624-6476; outside California 800 582-8900).

Completely restored and renovated in 1984, La Playa stands on what was the site of a rockwork mansion built by artist Chris Jorgensen for his bride, a daughter of the Ghirardelli family, back in 1911.

With its pink Mediterranean look and flower-filled grounds, La Playa appears to have just been transplanted from the South of France. Yet, only two blocks away there is Carmel's sandy, but most often breezy beach; four blocks away the heart of Ocean Avenue shopping. And when exhausted from lugging all your purchases back to the hotel, you can always pop into the pool. Some, but not all, of the gracefully appointed rooms have a view out toward the ocean.

My third recommendation is not in Carmel at all but in Monterey slightly north. The Monterey Plaza Hotel, 400 Cannery Row, Monterey, (California 800-334-3999; outside California 800-631-1339) is subtitled "The Grand Hotel on the Bay". And while it does try to fashion itself that way—impressive lobby with cocktail area and requisite pianist—it doesn't always succeed. But its big plus for me is its location directly on Monterey Bay, just a few blocks from the Monterey Aquarium and right on a hiking-jogging-bicycling path that can take you for miles along the scenic water's edge. However, I would only stay here if I could obtain a room overlooking the bay, and preferably one with a small balcony.

Now with confirmed reservations in hand, let's look to our packing. With ten championship golf courses (both public and private) and over a dozen tennis clubs (mostly public) in the Carmel-Monterey area, the requisite sports equipment is your first what-to-take consideration. You will also want to throw in some comfortable shoes for your shopping forays and for climbing over the many steps at Hearst's Castle.

While Carmel is "country casual" tweedy in dress, men might want to take a tie—just in case. The entire area is renowned for its benignly pleasant (although, at times, foggy) climate. So pack accordingly and if you forget to pack something you can always buy it in Carmel—no matter what "it" may be!

10:00 a.m.   After a fine breakfast at Sears' or in your hotel, start off by locating Sixth Street. Head south on Sixth Street and where it ends, drive directly up the entrance ramp to Highway 280.

Actually, the most direct route to our destination would be to take Highway 101 for about 90 miles before turning off onto Highway 156 for the Monterey Peninsula. Doing so, however, presents an unattractive landscape, tracing the Bay's western perimeter through dull industrial areas for the first 50 some miles. Since this stretch is also the primary commercial avenue to and from San Francisco, and passes the airport, the traffic can be fairly heavy.

Therefore, I suggest Highway 280, following the signs first to Daly City, then to San Jose.

You will first cut through the southern residential portion of San Francisco, then sweep gently up through the hillside bedroom communities of San Mateo County, overlooking the Bay. Soon you will be viewing some lovely hillscapes, with the waters of the Crystal Springs Reservoir glimmering in the sun. Then on through the horse-loving community of Woodside, skirting behind Stanford University and connecting up with 101 just south of San Jose.

Now follow the signs indicating "Highway 101, Los Angeles." This drive takes you through rich farmlands, past prune orchards and grape fields, increasingly threatened by the encroachment of suburban sprawl. About 50 miles later, take the turnoff to Highway 156 West, marked "Monterey Peninsula."

Suddenly, you will find yourself in the "Artichoke Capital of the World" with acres upon acres of the thistle-like plants stretching to the horizon. Highway 156 then swings into Highway 1 South, which will be the main artery of your travels for the next three days.

For those staying at the Monterey Plaza, as you approach Monterey watch for a right turnoff marked "Del Monte Ave (Pacific Grove)". Take it and simply follow the signs to the "Aquarium," until you have exited from a tunnel. Then make the first right onto Foam Street which then swings left onto Cannery Row. The Monterey Plaza is dead ahead.

For those who opted for La Playa, continue down Highway 1 past the Monterey exits until you reach Ocean Avenue. Turn right onto Ocean, passing through the main section of Carmel, turning left onto Camino Real for two blocks.

For those of you going to the Tickle Pink, just remain on Highway 1 as it by-passes Monterey and do *not* take any of the Carmel exits. About four miles south of Carmel, watch for a sign on the left indicating the Highlands Inn; then 800 feet later, turn left into its rising driveway, which is marked "Highlands Drive." Continue on up the drive, passing through the Highlands Inn's parking lot on to the Tickle Pink, right next door.

Now with all of us ensconced in our hotel rooms, thoughts might turn to food. With the drive down from San Francisco taking anywhere from 2 1/2 to 3 hours, depending on traffic, it should be nearing 1:00 p.m.

I haven't any specific suggestions for right now except to suggest caution. Tonight's dinner will be in my current favorite Carmel restaurant which has an exciting menu from appetizers to desserts.

However, if you would like a small snack, both the Monterey Plaza and La Playa serve lunch. For those at the Tickle Pink, you might just wander next door to the Highlands Inn and lunch there or pick up some sandwiches from their deli—the California Market (closed Mondays) —to take back to the Tickle Pink for lunch overlooking the sea.

2:00 p.m.   Now regardless of where you are situated, it's time to put your priorities in order—Mother Nature or shopping. Let's take the latter, first.

If you crave an afternoon of shopping, the place you are looking for is Ocean Avenue in downtown Carmel. Here, you will not require my guidance—just good walking shoes, a deck of credit cards, and a parking space. If you skipped lunch and are now regretting it, walk over to Patisserie Boissiere on Mission Street, between Ocean and 7th, for tea or coffee and a piece of French pastry.

To reach the shopping center of Carmel, from the Hotel La Playa only means a walk of a few blocks to be in the heart of the action. From the Tickle Pink, just drive back up Highway 1 for four miles then turn left down Ocean Avenue. For Monterey Plaza guests, turn left on exiting the hotel to Reeside Street. Right on Reeside and two blocks later left onto Lighthouse. Then just before the tunnel entrance, turn right onto Pacific Avenue, following Pacific to Highway 1 South to Carmel, where you turn right on Ocean.

Now then, if shopping doesn't appeal to you and you would rather experience, at close hand, a little of that marvelous meeting of land and sea that surrounds this entire area, I suggest you take a short drive to Point Lobos State Reserve.

Regarded by many as one of the most beautiful pieces of California coast, this 1,500-acre park boasts a 6-mile shoreline, along which you can hike and explore the incredible world of tide pools. During low tide, these pools are exposed and in them are microcosms of life —starfish, hermit crabs, sea urchins and sea anemones. Squatting by one of the pools and witnessing the beauty within, can mesmerize me for hours.

Point Lobos State Reserve is located on Highway 1 north of the the Tickle Pink and south of the town of Carmel.

However, if you are staying at the Monterey Plaza, and you don't want to get back into the car right now, you can still enjoy the seaside right within walking distance of your hotel. For almost outside your door is a special paved track for hikers, bicyclers, runners, joggers, and just plain walkers.

If you walk to the left—toward Monterey—you will soon come to its famed Fisherman's Wharf. Like most of these once colorful areas, it has now become "touristy" in the worst possible sense. They must make enough caramel corn here to feed the nation! (By the way, as you approach the Wharf, on your right you will spot Kiewel's Cafe, which serves a respectable breakfast on its big umbrella-shaded deck.)

However, if on leaving the hotel you turn right, you soon find yourself heading toward the seaside community of Pacific Grove. Your path takes you right alongside the lapping waters of Monterey Bay. On the nearby rocks you will see basking seals, their barking vying with the shrill cries of the gulls. Oh yes, those gull cries will be your wake-up call tomorrow morning, if you have a waterside room at the Plaza. Hope you like sun-up calls.

On the other side of the road are the homes of Pacific Grove. Their architectural style runs the gamut from tiny cottages, dating from the time this town was a Methodist encampment, through gingerbread Victorian up to sterile modern.

A fun way to traverse this route is by renting a "surrey." These four-wheeled, pedal-propelled contraptions hold two or three riders with maybe a toddler or two in the front basket. Of course, these surreys have fringe on top!

5:30 p.m. Time to think about returning to your hotel and enjoying the view from your room with a late afternoon cocktail. (If you are in Carmel and wish to take back some cocktail fixings with you, stop in at the superb Mediterranean Market at Ocean and Mission Streets.)

7:30 p.m. Time to head for dinner. Armed with an advance reservation, you will find this evening's destination on the east side of Highway 1 off Rio Road.

Rio Grill, The Crossroads, Route 1 and Rio Road, Carmel

(408-625-5436; open daily for lunch and dinner; reservations advised), is an exceptionally fine California-style grill, similar to Mustards which you may have encountered in the wine country and to which it was once financially related.

The atmosphere is open, airy, informal. The linen table cloths are covered with paper sheets and color crayons are provided as boredom-breaker doodling tools for tots or grown-ups.

But when the young and good-natured serving staff starts bringing you your orders, all attempts at art are aborted. For here in front of you can be placed a joyous garden-fresh tomato soup, thick with all sorts of minuscule vegetables, and slightly creamed. On one occasion the fried squid appeared slightly pale, but the texture of these circlets was perfect—not the rubber bands so often encountered—and the tartar sauce perkily piquant.

The intriguing menu—with all kinds of tempting side dishes and condiments—allows you to construct a mix-or-match meal to suit you own tastes. But remember you are in artichoke country, so try to include one of these tasty thistles, chaperoned by a roma-tomato relish and pesto mayonnaise.

And when on one visit, our expert waitress apologized for not being able to serve us any of their generally top-notch onion rings—the onions were too watery at that time of year for fine frying—I indulged in a dazzling daily pasta. Here was hearty penne all dolled up in cream, pinkish with pumate tomatoes, and festooned with sprigs of cilantro. *Che bella*!

For the main event, how about a delicious tenderloin porterhouse, tenderly marinated in vinegar, pepper corns, cilantro and hot peppers, and then grilled to a medium-rare perfection? Served with it are something closely resembling O'Brien potatoes—sensational. A thick veal chop is charred—almost New Orleans style—on the outside and fork-tender within, flavored with sprigs of rosemary and served with excellent polenta.

Desserts tend to be all-American classics with caloric

twists. A vanilla cheesecake combines the cheesiness of a New York version with the velour of a Bavarian. The chocolate brownie is scrumptuous and the ice cream on top has a real, vanilla bean flavor.

The wine list is faithful to California with some real winners like a *big* Ridge, York Creek, 1984 Cabernet Sauvignon. My notes from my last visit end with: "Everyone around us was ohing and ahing!" And so will you.

SECOND DAY

8:00 a.m. If the name of your game is golf, you will probably want the earliest cup of coffee you can order at your hotel and head out to the links. If golf is not your game, it certainly is the game of the Carmel-Monterey Peninsula, where fourteen courses award it the title "Golf Capital of the World." You may never have held a putter in your hands, but it is almost certain you have seen photos of the incredible 16th hole at Cypress Point, 220 yards of blue Pacific between tee and green.

Tennis is another favored recreation here and the area is dotted with courts. To ensure either golf or tennis availability, it is best to check with your travel agent or golf and tennis clubs at home.

If you do not wish to spend this morning on the greens or the courts, I have a few suggestions. If you spent yesterday afternoon at Point Lobos, perhaps you are ready to poke around Carmel's shops this morning. Or, you might take a journey back in time to the beginnings of Carmel by visiting the mission officially known as the Basilica San Carlos Borromeo del Rio Carmelo. This historic link with California's past and the final resting place of Father Junipero Serra, the founder of California's chain of missions, is located off Highway 1 to the west on Rio Road.

Or, you might wish to just beachcomb along a sandy beach, depending on what the fog is doing. If you do go, take your camera along to capture the photogenic wind-tortured cypress trees.

About now, you should give some consideration to

where, or rather, how you wish to lunch. As usual, I have a couple of recommendations. The first is a picnic along the north shore of the famed 17-Mile Drive; the second, an excellent and inexpensive Mexican cantina in historic Monterey, where you should spend the afternoon. But because seeing the 17-Mile Drive is mandatory for every first-time visitor to the area, let's start off by heading back to Ocean Avenue in Carmel.

11:00 a.m.   Drive down Ocean Avenue. (If you opted for the picnic, purchase whatever provisions you desire at the Mediterranean Market right on Ocean Avenue. They do not make sandwiches here, but they do have a great variety of coldcuts, cheeses, salads and breads. And you can also buy those little plastic packs of mustard, mayo, etc. at the cashier. The Mediterranean also has a huge wine selection. And don't forget some pastries from Patisserie Boissiere.)

Proceed down Ocean Avenue until you just about reach the beach, turning right on San Antonio Street at the "17-Mile Drive" sign. Pass through the gate (a $5.50 per auto charge for non-residents); ask for a map; and take the first left, ignoring the "17-Mile Drive" marker. Then pick up the red-dashed center line, marking your course through the drive.

Actually, you will only be traversing about half of the entire 17 miles, but it is by far the more scenic half. Within minutes, the famed Pebble Beach Golf Links will be on your left. (By the way, the Club XIX at the Lodge serves quite good lunches from tables overlooking the 18th hole and the Pacific beyond.)

Ranked in the top 10, this course serves as the home of the AT&T (formerly the Bing Crosby) Pro-Am Tournament each January. Then you will cut through an exclusive colony of mansions, erected in every imaginable style from Moorish to Modern to Colonial, yet they all have one thing in common—great wealth.

Out on a wind-swept point you will view "Lone Cypress," possibly the most painted and photographed tree in all America. Then comes the Cypress Point Club (private) and Fanshell Beach, a crescent of white sand where you can enjoy your picnic. Just a little further on (an ideal after-lunch walk), you will come upon Seal and Bird Rocks, the habitat of shore birds, sea lions and sea otters. Whatever you do, stop here for a few minutes to watch and listen to the hordes of sea lions on the offshore rocks.

Continuing on the 17-Mile Drive, watch for the sign marked "Pacific Grove Gate" and turn left. Soon you will exit the toll portion of the Drive and as you continue ahead the 17-Mile Drive becomes an ordinary quiet suburban street.

If the time of your visit happens to be in October or early November, I urge you to turn right onto Pine Street for two blocks. For on the corner of Grove Street and Pine is a small grove of trees which serve as the winter home for Monarch butterflies; enormous clusters of them are best visible in the afternoon sun.

Otherwise, continue along the 17-Mile Drive to Lighthouse Avenue, turn left. Where Lighthouse comes to a dead-end, swing right onto Asilomar Blvd., and where it dead ends at the edge of Monterey Bay turn right onto Ocean View.

Ocean View winds along the northern bayside edge of the town of Pacific Grove. Remain on Ocean View as it soon parallels the walking-bicycling course that I described a few pages back. At David Street, turn left and immediately you will be in front of the Monterey Bay Aquarium at David and Cannery Row.

Even if you do not particularly like zoos or aquariums, I urge you not to miss this spectacular exhibit. So you should stop and see if they have any tickets available during your stay, unless you have made prior arrangements, which are certainly advisable.

You see, since it opened in late 1984, the Monterey Bay Aquarium has become one of California's most popular attractions and tickets usually must be ordered in advance. However, again assuming you are reading ahead, let me fill you in on how you can experience this incredible structure.

In San Francisco tickets can be purchased in advance through Ticketron by calling 392-SHOW or by writing to them at P.O. Box 26430, San Francisco, CA 94126. Tickets are currently $8 for adults; $3.50 for children age 3-12; $5.75 for seniors. There is also a small service charge.

What was once an old fish canning factory has been transformed into a miraculous display of marine life, not in the usual tiny porthole-sized viewing chambers, but in towering sea-life galleries. Here the visitor has an eye-to-eye view of nearly 5,000 creatures that live in Monterey Bay. Children will especially love the hands-on exhibits where they can touch starfish and even bat rays.

On my first visit, I thought I would do a cursory run-through just to see if I should recommend it to you. Over two hours later I emerged absolutely exhilarated.

But right now let's proceed down Cannery Row, immortalized by John Steinbeck as "a poem, a stink, a grating noise." Today most of those original attributes have been replaced by their modern-day equivalents.

The noise today is from the hordes of visitors, especially youths, attracted to the honky-tonk atmosphere of the street. Almost all the ancient, weather-worn canneries have been converted into modern warrens of shops, restaurants, art galleries, etc. And tourists pack them as tightly as their previous occupants—the sardines! And instead of the stink of fisheries, the gas fumes of tour buses now blend with the saccharine smells of freshly-made hot fudge and popcorn. It is not my favorite part of town.

Soon Cannery Row turns right into Drake St. Continue up Drake to Lighthouse, where you turn left. Lighthouse Ave. will take you through the Military Reserve and, via a tunnel, into downtown Monterey.

Immediately on emerging from the tunnel, veer right onto Tyler, then left onto Franklin and, one block later, turn right onto Washington which soon becomes Abrego.

If you have picnicked or had lunch elsewhere, you may wish to park along here and take a walking tour of the old section of Monterey. If you wish to enjoy a fine Mexican cantina, remain on Abrego, past the stop light at Fremont.

A half block later on the right is a small sign marking Los Hermanos. Pull into the parking area adjacent to it.

Los Hermanos, 724 Abrego Street, Monterey (408 372-1032; open daily except Sunday for lunch until 3:00 and dinner), is the kind of restaurant I would love to have in San Francisco. Not necessarily for its physical appearance—a big barn of a place, done in light pink with a lot of plants and a tiny sun-baked patio. But for its excellent Mexican cuisine. In far too many Mexican restaurants in San Francisco, the food is slapdash. As if no one should take pains preparing a type of cuisine most people only consider when they want to "eat cheap."

But I love good Mexican cooking. And that is just what "The Brothers" provides—and at modest prices.

For example, the guacamole is perfection—not a hyper-blenderized faceless soup, but chunky with pieces of avocado and tomatoes and even bits of sweet onion. The requisite tortilla chips are thin, crisp and fresh from the frying fat.

The sopes are sensational. Each order consists of egg-shell-thin, handmade corn tortillas, deep fried and then stuffed with either a ground beef or chicken filling (both superbly spiced: although I prefer the beef), all topped with a tomato-onion salsa, shredded cabbage, sour cream and cheese. When I asked why shredded cabbage and not the usual lettuce, the waitress quickly replied that lettuce tends to wilt. And since the green is more important for texture than for flavor, sturdier cabbage works better.

Los Hermanos adds "con mariscos" to its title, which means with seafood. And when I ordered the camarones guajillos, I was presented with beautifully sweet sauteed prawns with red bell pepper-chile butter. Served with excellent rice and beans, it was an impeccable dish.

Yet, even more intriguing was the seafood cone taco, in which the restaurant specializes. The soft taco cone is filled with freshly cooked beans and your choice of prawns, bay snapper, crab or even chicken. I opted for the prawns and reveled in their sea-fresh flavor set off by sour cream, guacamole and guajillo salsa.

Naturally, Mexican beer is requisite for washing down this truly excellent cooking.

A short aside: back up in the Bay Area, my favorite Mexican restaurant is not in San Francisco but across the Bay Bridge in Oakland. It's called La Mexicana and is located at 3930 East 14th Avenue. In this plain-wrapper, storefront eatery with its formica-topped tables, the happy slapping sound of fresh tortillas being hand-crafted fills the air and some of the finest Mexican cuisine—yes, that term is perfectly applicable here—can fill your heart with joy!

Whether or not you lunch at Los Hermanos, Abrego Street is a good spot from which to launch a small walking tour of Old Monterey. The visitor's free monthly magazine, *This Month*, usually prints the route of a historic tour in each issue which you can use as a handy guide. And the Monterey State Historic Park office at 525 Polk Street (closed Wednesday) has a four-color brochure on Monterey's historic downtown. To reach the office, just walk back down Abrego Street, turning left on Polk for a couple of blocks. Copies of this pamphlet are also available at the offices of the Monterey Peninsula Chamber of Commerce, 380 Alvarado Street.

During this walk you will pass several historic adobes, many dating from 1830, including the Stevenson House, once the home of Robert Louis Stevenson, which contains a collection of memorabilia dating to 1879. Local Stevenson scholars like to point out that the geography of Point Lobos is remarkably similar to that of Stevenson's fictional *Treasure Island*.

Also along the walk you will come upon the Larkin House (daily guided tours), a perfect example of the "Monterey style" of architecture which had its beginnings as Spanish adobe (early 1800's) but was later modified by the New England seamen with the addition of a second story and a balcony.

Colton Hall on Pacific Street, built in 1847-49, is possibly the finest of the remaining old buildings. Other interesting structures along the route are the Custom House, the oldest government building on the Pacific Coast; and

California's First Theater (1846-1847) with its display of theatrical souvenirs from the past.

How much time you spend viewing and visiting these historic buildings depends upon your interest and perhaps the weather. If it is a fine day, this walk is an extremely pleasant way to assimilate some history while enjoying the sun. When you have soaked up enough of both, simply find your way back to Abrego Street, your car and your hotel.

6:00 p.m. Hopefully on your last night in Carmel-Monterey, there is a glowingly multi-hued sunset over the Pacific and your hotel room has a deck from which to enjoy it.

My dinner recommendation this evening is in Monterey. And because traffic on Highway 1 can be slow, I suggest that if you are staying at either the Tickle Pink or La Playa you allow plenty of time to arrive in time at your destination—The Whaling Station, 763 Wave Street near Cannery Row, Monterey, (408 373-4248; open nightly; reservations advised). If you are staying at the Monterey Plaza Hotel, you can walk the few short blocks in minutes.

Coming from Carmel or the Tickle Pink, drive north on Highway 1, passing Carmel to the Munras turnoff. Keep on Munras, then onto Alvarado to Del Monte. Left on Del Monte two blocks to Pacific, and right on Pacific, picking up signs to Cannery Row.

8:30 p.m. As is often the case in areas that attract a great number of tourists, restaurants in the Carmel-Monterey area undergo quick and often violent changes. What was a dazzling "in" Milanese-style restaurant of a few seasons ago, suddenly starts putting out lackluster pasta. A charming garden spot that once produced lovely fresh dishes goes to seed with lame micro-waved plates. And so it goes.

But the Whaling Station sails on. I don't want to imply that this a great restaurant. No, but it's a darned good one. Here overriding emphasis is on fresh fish, simply prepared. Now, most fish restaurants claim that is their goal, too. What makes the Whaling Station different is that they stick to their word. They don't augment their menu with a freezer chest of frozen seafood, even when the weather prevents the fishing fleet from bringing in the catch! And they show style in a number of other ways.

The moment you are seated you are presented with *the* vegetable of the area—a beautifully cooked, cold artichoke, in its center an herbed mayonnaise and a vinaigrette. Soups tend to be handsomely executed with some type of fish chowder usually on the stove. An interesting standby is a fine lightly creamed curried chicken.

Next comes a house salad the likes of which you would expect from a tony ala carte San Francisco eatery such as Stars. A variety of crisply fresh young leaves in a slightly sweet dressing of rice vinegar, honey and sesame seed oil, all garnished with cajun-spiced walnut pieces.

Actually, on my last visit I had momentary worries over the addition of some trendy newcomers to what was once a staid fish-house menu. But the sauteed foie gras was superbly managed—the fresh duck liver perfectly sauteed and served warm over a bed of crinkly greens in a light vinaigrette.

For a main course I suggest you stick to the tried and true fresh fish, grilled over oakwood and mesquite charcoal. It will be fresh; it will be good. Also, here is the place to encounter that now elusive mollusk, the abalone. I ask for it breaded and also request that the superfluous sprinkling of grated cheese be omitted.

Vegetables are always fresh and often offbeat, such as the sprightly dandelion greens served one evening or fresh asparagus spears atop red cabbage. Desserts tend to be run-of-the-mill.

The wine list, however, is not. And features the output of many Monterey County vintners. And it was on this list that I uncovered what has become my favorite California Chardonnay—Talbott. In fact, I was so enamored of it, that I purchased a case direct from the winery located a short drive away. By the way, if the name Talbott rings a bell, it is indeed the same family that produces one of Carmel's most famous products—Talbott neckties.

10:00 p.m. Better head back to your motel, you have a long drive tomorrow.

THE THIRD DAY

Your last chance to get in a morning of golf or tennis, or to make up your mind if that seascape painting you spotted in that Carmel side-street gallery would really suit the den wall. Then, it is packing and setting off down the coast.

Perhaps on your numerous treks back and forth along Highway 1 near Carmel, you may have noticed a rather ominous sign on the roadside heading south reading: "Curves and hills next 74 miles."

To those unaccustomed to California's coastal terrain, I want to impress upon you just what that means. It means that Highway 1, your approach to Hearst's Castle at San Simeon, will be at many times a two-lane roller coaster, clinging precariously to the sheer sides of the Santa Lucia Mountains with only a few feet of gravel and maybe a low stone wall between you and the Pacific Ocean a couple hundred feet below.

Even though I have covered this stretch many times, I would not traverse it in fog, rain or dark of night. I certainly do not want to frighten you out of this important leg of your trip because the rewards in unique scenery and Hearst's Castle are well worth the effort. But you should be aware of what lies ahead.

11:00 a.m. Find your way to Highway 1 and head south. Our lunch destination (about 30 miles south of Carmel) can be reached in 40 minutes, so you have plenty of time to take it easy, pulling onto some of the numerous turnouts on the right to better contemplate the vast panorama. Words fail to accurately describe this powerful meeting of land mass and surging sea—a symphony in itself which is called Big Sur Country.

12:00 noon.   By this time, you should be at Nepenthe, Highway 1, Big Sur (408 667-2345; open daily for lunch and dinner), where you will be having lunch.

Aptly named after the mythical drug which possessed the magical power to induce forgetfulness of sorrow, Nepenthe is far more than just a place to eat—it is a state of mind. The moment I arrive, I immediately cast off "city concerns" and my mind begins to quietly flow with the sweep of the mountains that curve into the sea.

Here, 800 feet above the Pacific, you are in another world, one without worries, one that is an extension of nature. The restaurant blends into its environment with its use of bare beams and adobe. The original building was the honeymoon cottage Orson Welles built for his bride, Rita Hayworth, in the '40s. And although the structure has been expanded greatly and now includes a two-story gift-and-handicraft shop, the entire complex remains totally unobtrusive.

The food Nepenthe serves is created in the same vein. Simplicity is the keynote, and the finest quality is the accepted norm. As you laze on the outside terrace overlooking the massive coastline to the south, you will swear your "Ambrosia Burger" is the finest you have ever enjoyed. The kosher pickle crackles and the bean salad beams with sprightly herbs.

French fries must be ordered separately and are cooked to order. I regard them as the ultimate in fries—crispy, golden and irresistible. And what a delight to find tea (no tea bag, either!) as beautifully brewed as it would be in a Mayfair drawing room. Sit here awhile and sip in silence. Nepenthe is to be slowly savored. It is a unique place.

1:45 p.m.   I am always loathe to leave Nepenthe, to quit its hold on my senses, to take leave of the peaceful aura radiated by the Big Sur regulars who gather here, using it as a social and cultural center. But. . . we must leave.

We are headed to one of the most mind-boggling displays of ostentatious power and wealth in America. The drive to Hearst's Castle proper covers less than 60 miles, most of it being curves and hills. It should take over 2 hours, depending on stops. Speaking of stops, an important one for those interested in the creativity of the Big Sur Colony, is the Coast Gallery, south of Nepenthe on the left.

As you approach San Simeon, you can spot the massive complex of buildings on the crest of a hill several miles off in the distance, looming above the countryside like some wild creation of Bavaria's mad King Ludwig. Your overnight lodgings lie about 6 1/2 miles further south, but you may wish to pull into the Castle's tourist center in order to pick up a brochure on the history and contents of the place.

The best way to avoid finding that tours to the Castle are all sold out on the day you arrive is to purchase your tickets in San Francisco before departing for San Simeon. Tickets for any of the three different major tours (see below for descriptions) are available by phone (800 444-7275).

Failing to obtain your Hearst Castle tickets in San Francisco, you should purchase them at the Castle on the afternoon of your arrival for the earliest available tours the next morning.

As of this writing, all three of the tours are guided. No cars are allowed up at the Castle; you are bused there from a tourist station down off Highway 1.

Tour #1 includes the swimming pools, one guest house, the garden, and the ground floor of the Castle itself. Tour #2 shows you the pools, garden, upper level of the Castle and the kitchen. Tour #3 takes in the pools, garden and guest rooms of the North Wing.

Tour #1 is the one I recommend for all first-time visitors, but I have found some of the rooms on Tour #2 extremely interesting, especially the Celestial Suite filled with a magical light created by the sun filtering through the filligree-carved shutters. Naturally, the kitchen holds a special place in my interests!

There is little reason for me to devote much time to details on the Castle or its contents. The complimentary brochure and your well-schooled guides will give you plenty of facts and figures. All I can and should say is that you are due for an intriguing experience. I had thought from my reading that all of it was grotesque and in poor taste. So I was in for a surprise on my initial visit.

Here are some magnificent antiques—tapestries especially—even if intermixed with little regard for their aesthetic effect on one another, to say nothing of an utter disregard for chronology.

The most surprising thing, however, is that the Castle—designed by Julia Morgan, whose works can also be seen in San Francisco and Berkeley—was not created as a stuffy museum but as the actual, comfortable residence of one man. I think this is the thing which astonishes most visitors.

Big, inexpensive, floral-covered over-stuffed chairs are scattered in rooms containing ceilings worth hundreds of thousands of dollars. This, too, comes up for much criticism. Yet, one must keep in mind that floral overstuffed chairs were much in vogue in the days the Castle was being furnished and, whether they are in good taste or not, they certainly look comfortable and inviting. In fact, all the rooms look livable despite the inclusion of some startling antique pieces.

A trip to Hearst's Castle would be worth it for the outdoor swimming pool alone. I doubt if you will ever see anything like it again in American architecture. It is breathtakingly beautiful. (If you experience *deja vu* while taking in its blue depths and white-pillared border, then you probably saw the movie *Spartacus* in which it served as the set for a Roman Emperor's bath.)

Add to this the great variety of flowers and fruit trees which are especially magnificent in the spring, and you will have a two-hour tour you will long remember.

After stopping at the Castle's tourist center to pick up an illustrated brochure, simply continue further down Highway 1 for 6 1/2 miles to Moonstone Beach Drive, turning right to San Simeon Pines, (805) 927-4648.

When I first came to visit the Castle, there were only two

or three motels in the area. But now that it is one of the major attractions in the state, box after box of faceless motels line the highway.

The Pines is by no means elegant or luxurious— although some rooms have fireplaces—but it is not one of those faceless blockhouses. The staff is friendly and accommodating; the setting quite charming—there is even a croquet pitch! And a few yards away is a state seashore park. Here you can shuffle aimlessly along the sandy beach, or sit up on the bluff among the cypress awaiting the descent of the sun into the vast Pacific. It is an ideal place to stretch your legs after the tension of the Highway 1 drive.

When you check into the Pines, ask the clerk to place a dinner reservation for you at Rigdon Hall, 4022 Burton Drive, Cambria, (805 927-5125; open nightly for dinner; reservations advised).

Rigdon Hall is a big, buoyantly friendly place with good, satisfying food. The soup can be a mulligatawny, an honest chicken-curry-tomato melange, served piping hot. Your salad will be nicely crisp greens tossed with a commendable Italian-style vinaigrette.

For main courses, their sirloin steak with a Dijon sauce is expertly handled as is a Spencer steak, which has been bathed in bourbon, Jack Daniels to be precise. The dessert selection includes a far-above-average cheesecake brought in from Los Angeles.

The wine list includes a remarkable variety of modestly-priced local—Paso Robles area—wines and the dining room staff is surprisingly quite well versed in them. Try something like the Eberle Cabernet. Not an award winner but quite good at the price. And that sums up the restaurant, too!

THE FOURTH DAY

Hopefully, you were able to purchase tickets to a fairly early morning tour of the Castle. So the best course of action is to pack up the car first, check out and head north to the Castle.

After you have witnessed Mr. Hearst's home and pondered a bit on the immense wealth that allowed him to construct it, you are ready to end your excursion and to return to San Francisco. You do not have to face tortuous Highway 1 again. There is a very simple route back. It will not give you the incredible scenic wonders of the Big Sur Coast, but its four-lane freeway construction certainly will be welcomed.

However, you might wish to stop first for breakfast, since the freeway back to the Bay Area offers little more than Big Macs. And in Cambria, there is an excellent place called Creekside Gardens Cafe, 2114 Main Street, Cambria (805 917-8646; open daily for breakfast and lunch). "Let us pamper you with food mother wished she'd made" is a sign that greets you. And indeed they do come up with excellent orange juice, fine pancakes, great bacon and good coffee. And the serving staff rivals that at Rigdon Hall for sheer unbridled friendliness.

Now to head back to Bay Area, just drive south on Highway 1. (If you have enjoyed breakfast at the Creekside, continue on Main street through the old town and you will hit Highway 1 South in about a mile.)

Once on Highway 1 South, turn left again on Highway 46. And after 20 miles of smooth, gradually graded roadway rising to some 1,700 feet above verdant farmlands, you will connect with Highway 101 North. In about 3 1/2 to 4 hours, you will be back in San Francisco. However, the first one who says, "That Hearst Castle is a great place to visit, but I wouldn't want to live there" walks!

If, after your long drive back to San Francisco, you want to just settle for a room-service dinner in your hotel, I can't really blame you. I know the feeling all too well! On the other hand, because there was no scheduled lunch stop, a visit to a restaurant that serves a cuisine unlike any you had on your trip might be just the thing. And since it is not in the downtown area, your rental car comes in handy.

Garden House, 133 Clement Street near Third Avenue

(221-3655; open every night for dinner; lunch served on Saturday and Sunday), is another San Francisco restaurant which showcases the exhilarating cuisine of Vietnam. And its intriguing juxtapositions of flavors and textures are just what I crave after several days of basically American cuisine.

If you are familiar with Vietnamese cuisine, you will no doubt recognize many of its great classics on the Garden House menu. For example, their imperial rolls are among the very best in town. These rolls filled with pork, shrimp and crab are deep fried and served with cold vermicelli-thin noodles, mint leaves, coriander and a dipping sauce. You place a little of each of the condiments along with a piece of the fried roll into a piece of lettuce leaf, wrap it all up and dip it into the sauce. Delicious.

As I said in my recommendation of Golden Turtle earlier, Vietnamese appetizers are often the most exciting aspect of their cuisine, so do not hesitate in ordering several, such as their barbecued beef in chao fun. Into a thickish, gelatinous noodle (chao fun) are placed slightly spicy pieces of crispy barbecued beef and lettuce. I know it may sound a little strange, but what a wonderful study in flavor and texture contrasts. But perhaps my very favorite dish at Garden House is their remarkable raw beef salad in which the paper-thin slices of beef have been tossed in a fiery chili-peanut dressing.

For main courses, the chicken with lemon grass presents tender slices of chicken treated to a chili hot sauce, into which some coconut milk has been added. Garden House appears infallible when it comes to handling seafood, so be sure to try their broiled shrimp served on a bed of those vermicelli noodles or their crispy prawns, sauteed with a melange of barely cooked vegetables—cauliflower, snow peas, lettuce, onions, greenpeppers.

No wine for me with this kind of spicy cooking. I prefer the fire-extinguisher properties of beer. And even if you drink several of them—which you can be tempted to do, given the spiciness of some of the dishes—the check will still be well within the moderate range.

A Three-Day Trip to the Napa Valley

NOTE: The Sixth Day's schedule is a day's outing to the wine country, which covers some of the same area as this recommended three-day trip. Therefore, you may wish to refer to it, when making plans for this more extended visit.

Nearly thirty years ago when the very first edition of this book saw printer's ink, I would never have thought of including an overnight stay in the beautiful Napa Valley, California's most famous wine-producing area. The reason was simple: there were no really fine places to spend the night and even good, let alone great, dining spots were non-existent.

But now, that has all changed. Today, the Napa Valley can provide all kinds of accommodations from dozens of bed-and-breakfast nooks to deluxe resorts. There are hot-air balloon rides and a just-introduced Napa Valley wine train. And as for restaurants, the Valley now boasts of some that can rival the finest in San Francisco.

I doubt if there is any one single factor that can claim the distinction—dubious to many who loved the Valley's more peaceful former mien—of placing the Napa Valley high on the list of places for both local resident and tourist to visit.

Perhaps the gasoline crunch of the early '70s made San Franciscans finally realize that the Valley offered the peace, quiet and guaranteed warm summer days, which had made far more distant Lake Tahoe such a haven for generations.

And then there was television. When *Falconcrest* became a hit series, millions upon millions of Americans became aware of the Napa Valley and a lot of them wanted to see it and the actual *Falconcrest* house.

Well, while I have never seen *Falconcrest*—neither the

TV show nor the actual house—I too have become a regular Napa Valley goer. But my reasons are that it offers me dual pleasures—a wonderful place to relax and the opportunity to wine and dine splendidly—all within the reach of a tankful of gas.

But what about you? Should you plan a stay of a day or two in the Napa Valley? Well, do you like hot summer days which offer nothing more exciting than time to laze around a pool or visit some of the greatest wineries in America?

Do you enjoy the rural sights of a breathtakingly beautiful valley covered with mile upon mile of vines—where in the spring mustard grass carpets the fields in brilliant yellow, while in summer roses bloom at every turn?

Would you relish dining in small country restaurants in which masterful young chefs treat the finest of local ingredients with elan and enhance their presentations with the greatest lists of California wines in America?

Well, if you answered yes to any or all of the above, then you should plan a two-night stay in the Napa Valley.

But just where do you stay?

I have personally bedded down at several inns and hotels in the Valley. And rather than simply recommend one, I will tell you about the four I prefer and you can make up your own mind.

Auberge du Soleil, 180 Rutherford Hill Road, Rutherford, (707) 963-1211, certainly heads the list as one of the most luxurious. Situated in an olive grove on a hillside, the inn offers a view of the valley from each of its rooms and suites. Each also has a wet bar, fireplace and deck, from which on early mornings you can watch majestic multi-colored hot-air balloons drift lazily over the valley. (Ballooning is a big attraction in the Napa Valley, but more about that later.)

The decor of the rooms, especially the living areas of the suites, is superb. The inn also has a small but beautifully situated swimming pool as well as tennis courts and a sauna. My preference in rooms or a suite are those on the top floor of the lower terrace, such as the Lorraine (each is named after a province of France). But we are talking top dollar when we speak of the Auberge du Soleil. I can heartily recommend everything about this beautiful "Inn of the Sun" except the restaurant, where I find the cuisine to be a disappointment.

Therefore, if you stay at the Auberge, you might wish to try lunch to see if matters have improved in the kitchen. With such stunningly appointed accommodations and the Valley's best vantage point, the Auberge du Soleil should have an equally impressive cuisine.

The Wine Country Inn, 1152 Lodi Lane, St. Helena, (707) 963-7077, is the place to stay if you like real country-inn ambience. Located further north up the valley on a gentle slope, the inn looks as if it has been there for years. But it hasn't. It was just built to look that way.

Inside the rooms are cozy with bright, patterned materials used in profusion and pretty but not spectacular rural views. They are far removed from the trendy "decorated" rooms of the Auberge du Soleil. And don't bother to look for a phone or a TV set in the room, there are none. One concession to modern tastes—and a necessity on hot valley days—is a swimming pool. There is no restaurant, but complimentary continental breakfasts are served in the homey public room. An ideal spot for those who really like to get away.

The Vintage Inn, Yountville, (707) 944-1112 or toll free 800-9-VALLEY, was opened in the fall of 1985. It seems as though the designers were quite conscious of its prosaic location—right between the highway and the main street of Yountville—and tried to distract from that disadvantage with some very clever ploys. For example, a long artificial stream features several small fountains, their pleasant splash making you less aware of the traffic sounds from the very nearby main road.

The rooms are lavishly appointed in soothing colors, often incorporating shades of wine tones. Each has a fire-place and whirlpool bathtub. A plentiful continental breakfast with champagne is served in the public area, while there is a chilled bottle of wine in your room's refrigerator. The help is youthful and aims to please. But even with all this attention to detail, The Vintage Inn still seems to me to be a large motel, albeit a very comfortable, handsomely appointed and well designed one.

Harvest Inn, One Main Street, St. Helena, (707) 963-9463 or (800) 950-8466, is located right off Highway 29 at the southernmost end of St. Helena. And although the highway is just a few yards away, the situation of the buildings almost removes it from your consciousness.

The buildings—in a faux Tudor style—are surrounded with trees, lawns and flower beds. The rooms are extraordinarily spacious, most with brick fireplaces that resemble castles from some children's illustrated fairy story. My preference for rooms are those that overlook the mountains to the west.

So with advance reservations at one of these establishments or at some other place you have heard of, let's not waste any further time but get going.

There are two basic routes to the Wine Country. One is to leave San Francisco via the Bay Bridge. Then onto Highway 80 (marked Sacramento, Reno), crossing the Carquinez Bridge and then following signs to Napa.

However, I prefer the less congested and more rural route through Marin County. (This is also the recommended route for our one-day outing to the Wine Country on Day Six.)

Simply drive over the Golden Gate Bridge—finding it should offer you no problem by now!—and continue on up Highway 101 through Marin County.

About 20 miles north of the bridge, turn off onto Highway 37 (marked "Vallejo, Napa"). Seven and a half miles later, turn left onto Highway 121 (marked "Sonoma, Napa"). Remain on Highway 121 as it swings right (do not take Sonoma turnoff, as we did on Day Six), following the signs to Napa. Soon you will be passing through the rich Carneros Valley, which reaches down to the northernmost shores of San Pablo Bay. In what was once strictly dairyland, you will now see acres of vines vying with cow pastures. Simply continue on Highway 121 until it hits

Highway 29 at a traffic light. Turn left onto Highway 29, and head up the Napa Valley.

Highway 29 is the main artery of the valley, passing through the towns of Yountville, Rutherford and Saint Helena. Almost all the major restaurants and inns are located within a short distance off this road. However, during your stay up here—especially if it is on a crowded summer weekend—you might find the Silverado Trail, which parallels Highway 29 to the east, is a more pleasant avenue to use in travelling to restaurants and wineries. (By the way, the Auberge du Soleil in located off the Silverado Trail in Rutherford.)

As I said at the beginning of this chapter, there is very little to do in the Napa Valley except relax, so I will depart from my usual hour-by-hour agenda and simply make some general suggestions for activities but some very specific ones for dining.

Since the Napa Valley became "in," the restaurant scene has been enormously affected. During the summer, stretch limos disgorge San Francisco's most beautiful people at the latest trendy restaurant, suddenly "hot" although not necessarily because of the cuisine, while more worthwhile dining rooms are abandoned as "out."

For example, Miramonte and Le Rhone, two superb French restaurants recommended in the last edition of this guide, are no longer.

Nevertheless, there are some superb restaurants up here, so let's start with a place to dine for tonight. (Again, reservations must be made as far in advance as possible.)

Terra, 1345 Railroad Avenue, St. Helena (707 963-8931; dinner only nightly except Tuesday; reservations strongly advised), is certainly one of the finest restaurants today in the Napa Valley. Located in a stone building that was originally built as a foundry, the interior has a simple elegance. The beamed ceiling and perfect unobtrusive lighting give the wine cellar-like atmosphere the right balance between country casual and serious-dining formal. The help is expert without being obsequious. And most of these youngsters know more about California wines than many of their generations-older customers.

While the in vogue cuisine in the Valley is Italian, just as a few years ago it was strictly French, and Terra sounds like an Italian restaurant, it really isn't. The co-owner chef is Japanese and did duty under Wolfgang Puck of Los Angeles' Spago. And although the most famous dish is classic Italian, don't be surprised to find such items as a scallop tartar, barbequed eel with Japanese cucumber salad and other cultural cross-overs.

For openers, an Italian panzarotti outdoes anything like it I have ever tasted in Italy. The deep-fried pasta pillows melt on the tongue and the cheese filling is almost liquid. The tomato sauce which surrounds them is not the kind that was reduced to acid by stewing in a pan for hours, but freshly, openly, sweetly tomato.

The baked mussels in garlic-herb butter treats these mollusks as though they were snails. Encased in the indentations of a snail ramekin, the mussels are covered in the garlic-herb butter—with some flecks of tomato—and baked. As with escargot, sop up every bit of that melted butter with some of the greatest bread ever. I hear it comes from a bakery in Napa called Scambra. The butteriest baguette ever! Another stellar first course is a puff pastry filled with wild mushrooms and smoked bacon. (I understand co-owner Lissa Doumani did pastries for Puck at one time.)

There is always one soup offering and consider yourself lucky if it is something like a joyous whitebean and tripe stew.

For main courses, the osso buco with risotto Milanese is majestic. The veal slides from the shank at your fork's approach. The tomato sauce is perfection. And be sure to use the long narrow spoon to scoop out that precious bone marrow and mix it into your ideal saffron-scented rice. Another centerpiece can be grilled pork chops, obviously marinated in some mystery brew, and served with a feathery yam puree. The accompanying highly spiced onion salad suddenly reminds you of the chef's Japanese heritage.

The ginger creme brulee which covers pear slices—poached in their own liquid—can make macho men melt. But then the apple tarte with vanilla ice cream and apple-cider sauce is also irresistible. As is to be expected in this area, the wine list runs on for pages.

Many years ago, a master chef with Japanese origins by the name of Masa conquered the Napa Valley, and later San Francisco, with French cuisine that bore the indelible but not obtrusive stamp of his culinary heritage. Today, I find Hiroyoshi Sone of Terra doing the same thing. By investing many Italian dishes with a clarity of flavor and lightness, he creates a truly memorable cuisine all his own. (Oh yes, for similar preparations—or attempts at such—you would pay almost double the price in San Francisco.)

Trilogy, 1234 Main Street, St. Helena (707 963-5507; lunches Tuesday through Friday; dinners Tuesday through Saturday; reservations), is housed in what was formerly Le Rhone, a long-time favorite of mine. It is not as faithfully French as the former but rather incorporates some Italian and other ethnic accents into a sparkling, eclectic, multi-lingual cuisine.

No restaurant in France—or in Italy, for that matter—that I have ever come across serves such a magnificent fettuccine with mushrooms and garlic cream sauce. The pasta is freshly cooked, and the sauce sings with the essence of fresh mushrooms and the barest murmur of garlic. Another Italian accent is sounded in a quasi-salad dish of grilled quail, served on herbed polenta along with frisee lettuce in a light hazelnut dressing.

Soups are simply wondrous. For example, a velvety cream of celery root—a flavor which can be overbearing—was mellowed by the sweetness of leeks.

I was at first quite puzzled by the Florida rock shrimp wrapped in romaine. I assumed the dish would be hot and it wasn't. I was also taken aback by what seemed to be a Japanese-style dressing which appeared to combine citrus and sesame. But I was quickly won over by the intriguing combination of these diverse flavors.

For main courses, the sauteed medallions of veal possess

the requisite fork-tenderness, their innocent flavor enhanced by a restrained use of capers and lemon. A sauteed breast of chicken is consummately handled with a perky but not overpowering Dijon mustard sauce. The steamed halibut falls away in pristine white flakes, scented by threads of saffron and hints of chive and shallot.

While most "modern" French restaurants have retreated from overly garnished plates—perhaps a fan of snow peas and a single rose petal—Trilogy bestows upon each entree a full array of vegetables. And what is truly remarkable, is the absolutely precise handling of each of them. To make matters more complicated, the garnitures on each plate vary. For example, while the veal may be chaperoned by brilliantly green broccoli flowerets, purple brussel sprouts, whisper-thin zucchini slices, a whipped carrot puree and wild rice pilaf, the fish dish receives reed-thin asparagus spears, spaghetti squash, nut-flavored white rice, baby sweet peas, and the carrot puree. This mind-boggling variety would be difficult for a mammoth kitchen to accomplish with any style. But somehow Trilogy finds a way and succeeds almost to excess!

Desserts are equally splendid as, for example, a tart lemon tart and a devilishly-deep chocolate mousse cake. The wine list—with shockingly low (yes, low!) prices—runs on for pages, but is not stocked in depth. Therefore, when you make your selection—one of the owners is a walking oenology encyclopedia, so be sure to ask his advice—make certain they have more than a single bottle in stock if you think you might wish a second of the same.

Trilogy presents masterfully prepared dinners in a pleasant atmosphere at prices far below equivalent cuisine in San Francisco. And they augment their culinary artistry with a wine cellar which they offer at barely-above-retail prices. What more could anyone ask?

If Trilogy and Terra—within a block of each other in St. Helena—are my two favorite Napa Valley dinner spots, Mustards in Yountville is *the* place for lunch.

Mustards Grill, 7339 St. Helena Highway (Highway 29) just north of Yountville (707 944-2424; open daily for lunch and dinner; reservations best), greets you with a tangible sense of excitement from the moment you walk in the door. It is not just that the place will be crowded—it always is—but it simply exudes good vibes.

The dining area is attractive in a lean-clean way with enough art on the walls to save it from austerity. The menu is a prime example of California cuisine. So whatever is "in" culinarily at the moment will be listed. But it will also be handled with such grace and expertise as to elevate Mustards from the masses of such grills.

In fact, the people who operate Mustards are also responsible for several other restaurants—Fog City Diner, Bix and Roti in San Francisco, for example. Yet in none of these popular places have I found the incredible accuracy rate of kitchen success which is a hallmark of Mustards.

If you have dined at the Rio Grill, which I recommended for our Carmel-Monterey side trip and which first saw life as a Mustards sibling, you will recognize the menu style.

A string bean salad of blushingly young, raw *haricot verts* is tossed with smoked tomato and crumbled goat cheese and garnished with endive fingers. Rock shrimp popcorn are golden balls of the sweet Florida shrimp, deep fried to perfection and served with a spicy sherry-cayenne spiked mayonaise. A tissue-thin cornmeal pancake is topped with Tobiko caviar (red but excellent; not overly salty) and napped with creme fraiche. There is a Chinese chicken salad without the jerky-like shreds of dried chicken you often encounter, but with beautifully plump pieces. A minestrone is sunshine sweet with halved yellow tomatoes and filled with all manner of beans and even some barley. Outstanding!

For main courses, the calf's liver is creamy textured and partnered by mouthwatering carmelized onions. And speaking of onions, Mustards' angelhair onion rings are celestial. Another handsome side dish is grilled new potatoes, skins and all!

Champion main courses also include their Hoisin-style barbecued chicken, where the crisp-skinned fowl has been basted with the kind of sauce that one usually associates with Peking duck. Another temptation for barbecue lovers is their mighty friendly barbecued brisket sandwich!

For dessert there are fragile caramel custards with fresh berries, inordinately rich chocolate-pecan cakes, and the likes of apple brioche pudding. My, oh my! And as the sun beats down outside, the camaraderie—intensified by such potables as a Duckhorn Merlot '87—can reach such proportions that table neighbors will offer you samples of their particular favorite food. Mustards is the quintessential grill—a great place to eat, drink and have fun.

The only meal of the day I have left uncooked is breakfast, but the Napa Valley has a great place for that too!

The Diner, 6476 Washington Street, Yountville (707-944-2626; open Tuesday through Sunday for breakfast, lunch and dinner), is a colorful roadside eatery that serves up great breakfasts, some with a Tex-Mex accent.

Because of the heavy-duty dining to which I must subject myself, The Diner is my traditional breakfast stop on my last day in the valley before I face the drive home. The orange juice is freshly squeezed and you don't have to mortgage the ranch to pay for it, as you do in posh city hotels. You can have it mixed with champagne, if you are not driving.

The breads are outstanding. All baked on the premises, they make the French toast—utilizing a raisin-nut bread, for example—the thing to order. The cornmeal pancakes are great; the buttermilk pancakes of the thick fluffy variety. The coffee—from San Francisco's beloved Graffeo which has been perfuming the air of North Beach lo these many years—superb.

Well, now that I have made certain you are well fed during your Napa Valley stay, how about something other than dining.

If dining is my favorite Napa Valley activity, wining is right up there. And wine-tasting takes on the rigors of a marathon with literally dozens for some of America's—and the world's—great wineries welcoming you in their tasting rooms.

But here are some tips: let moderation be your guide.

And in travelling the length of the valley try to use the Silverado Trail rather than Highway 29. You will find it far less congested. And if you travel at times by bicycle, its bike path is wider than that of Highway 29. And whatever you do, don't miss Sterling Winery, one of the Valley's most spectacular (for full details, please see Day Six of this Guide).

Another pastime which has gained exceptional popularity in the Napa Valley has French roots, or rather wings. And that is hot-air ballooning.

Over 200 years ago, the brothers Montgolfier created the first hot-air balloon. And a duck, a rooster and a sheep became the world's first aviators. In today's jet age, many delight in returning to this original means of air travel. I have not been among them, but if you are interested here are a couple of firms willing to take you above the terra firma of the Napa Valley: Adventures Aloft, P.O. Box 2500, Yountville, CA 94599, (707) 255-8688; Balloon Aviation of Napa Valley, 2299 Third Street, Napa, CA 94558, (707) 252-7067.

A new attraction in the Napa Valley is the highly controversial Napa Valley Wine Train—controversial because many residents fought it long and hard on the grounds that it was too touristy and thus detrimental to the environment of this once bucolic valley.

But the burgundy and chablis-colored train finally got onto the tracks in 1989 and makes a 36-mile roundtrip (from Napa to St. Helena and back) several times a day. The three-hour journey is done at a snail's pace so that meals can be served in dining cars that look like something out of Europe's famed Orient Express.

I have yet to take the Wine Train, but if you like this up-close view of the valley, you might wish to try it. As of this moment and until an environmental impact study is released, passengers cannot get off anywhere along the route, but must make the full round trip.

If you think of trying the train, I would certainly recommend the brunch or lunch excursion when the valley can be appreciated in full daylight. For more information, you may write the Napa Valley Wine Train, 1274 McKinstry Street, Napa, CA 94559, or call (707) 253-2111 or (800) 522-4142. It might be a hoot!

But my preferred way of seeing some of the Napa Valley is in boots—hiking in Bothe-Napa Valley State Park, right off Highway 29 some three and a half miles north of St. Helena.

Here you will find a full-facility state park—picnic tables, camping sites (call 707-942-4575) and even a swimming pool (water temperature about 70 degrees in the summer).

But what draws me here are the lovely hikes one may take. There are easy ones, moderate ones and even a fairly strenuous one. All are well marked and there are maps available at the information office.

So you really don't need regulation hiking boots, but just sensible shoes to enjoy long walks through forests, including redwoods. But don't just keep you eyes skyward, gazing at the giant trees. Keep a careful lookout on the ground. For here, for example in March, you might see beautiful, rare calypso orchids growing wild. There are varieties of trillium, Solomon seal, hound's tongue and numerous others, depending on the time of year.

At the southern end of the park, again right off Highway 29, there is the Bale Grist Mill. Built in 1846, it has been restored to operating condition. And usually at one and four on weekend afternoons, the mill's 36-foot wooden waterwheel turns the enormous millstones and grinds out cornmeal. I never will forget walking into the old mill house one glorious March afternoon and being greeted by the aroma of baking cornbread. A woman in period costume was handing out samples. Wow! You talk about *haute cuisine*!

And finally, if you insist on visiting one of the valley's most popular sights, you will find *Falconcrest* at 2805 Spring Mountain Road.

When your wine-country stay must come to an end, head back to San Francisco by driving south on now very familiar Highway 29. At Napa pick up Highway 121 which will lead you to Highway 37, which, in turn, takes you to the Redwood Highway 101 and on to San Francisco.

After the rich food and award-winning wines you have been so mercilessly subjected to for the past few days, I don't think it would be humane of me to offer you anything even remotely similar. So on your return to San Francisco, allow me to introduce you to San Francisco's number one Hong Kong-style Chinese restaurant.

The Hong Kong Flower Lounge, 5322 Geary Blvd. near 17th Avenue (668-8998; open daily for lunch and dinner; reservations strongly advised), just opened as this book was being set in type. But I did not hesitate in including it because its parent operation in Millbrae (down near the airport) has been regarded as *the* ultimate Hong Kong restaurant for years. And that enormous operation is the Northern California outpost of a firm that operates several restaurants in the British Crown Colony.

What makes Hong Kong-style Chinese cuisine different? Well, first of all with Hong Kong being an island, there is great emphasis on seafood. And secondly, dishes appear to be less complex with fewer ingredients used in each dish. You achieve the texture and flavor contrasts by ordering dishes which complement each other.

And as you construct your dinner, here are some of the dishes you should certainly consider.

For starters, The Flower Lounge specializes in shark's fin and its shark's fin soup (quite costly) with shredded chicken is glorious. The somewhat gelatinous, darkish stock is beautifully flavored and the thin threads of translucent shark fin work well with the tender shreds of chicken.

The Peking duck is one of the best in town and you should order it when you call for your reservation. The meat is moist and the skin the requisite parchment crisp. Actually, I don't believe the fried prawns with walnuts in special sauce is old Hong Kong at all. Because when I saw the dish prepared on a Chinese TV cooking show, one of the major ingredients was good ole mayonnaise. But don't let the curious cross-over turn you off, these big, tasty prawns are wok sauteed then treated to a mayonnaise glaze that has been seriously flavored with mustard. The accompanying sweet-glazed walnuts are the ideal foil to set off their flavor.

On one visit, the deep-fried cat fish was unanimously voted "best dish." The outer skin was millimeters thin and crisp, while the white flesh inside was infinitely light. The pan-fried pork chops are wonderful—thinly sliced bone-in chops, dusted in an intriguing spice blend then quickly fried and served ungarnished. Minced squab, mixed with perhaps some nuts or water chestnuts, is also pan fried then placed upon a bed of dry rice noodles. You place this combo into cups of green lettuce leaves.

As you can see, except for the lettuce leaves, there has been no sign of a vegetable. So something like baby bok choy or asparagus in season is an ideal foil. On one visit, the latter was treated to what looked like an inordinate amount of chopped garlic. But it was miraculously sweet.

There are a couple of caveats about the Flower Lounge. Many of the young waiters speak and understand very little English. So, if you believe this is the case, help them understand you by pointing to the items on the menu. And even though you may not succeed, try to get your waiter to bring dishes in the order you desire. I have always believed that the erratic appearances of dishes in many Chinese restaurants is because the kitchens may gang similar orders from different tables. But try.

And finally, ask about dishes you do not see on the menu. Even though the menu has now been expanded to include more dishes formerly given only in Chinese, there are still many hidden delights. For example, at certain times of the year they prepare an incredible unlisted beef with mango.

But it's all worth the effort, because this is truly some of the best Hong Kong-style cuisine you will taste outside... Hong Kong.

To reach The Hong Kong Flower Lounge on returning from the Napa Valley, simply take the turn-off marked "19th Avenue; Highway 1" after you pass through the

Golden Gate Bridge toll plaza on the San Francisco side. This places you onto Park Presidio Drive. At the fourth stop light, turn right onto Geary Blvd. The Flower Lounge is on the right in about three blocks. After dinner, simply reverse your direction on Geary Blvd. and drive right back to the Union Square Area.

Index of Recommended Restaurants

This index covers all restaurants recommended in this book and, for your convenience, lists them by location and style of cuisine served. Because restaurants often change days and hours open, you are urged to phone ahead in all cases. And, except where they are not accepted, reservations are strongly advised. The description of the restaurant along with specific menu suggestions appear on the pages indicated.

Recommended Restaurants:

225

Tung Fong   20
808 Pacific Ave.
S.F.   362-7115

Whaling Station   201
763 Wave St.
Monterey   (408) 373-4248

Yuet Lee   40
1300 Stockton St.
S.F.   982-6020

Zola's   105
395 Hayes St.
S.F.   864-4824

Restaurants by Location:

WINE COUNTRY:

Diner, The
John Ash & Company
Mustards
Piatti
Terra
Trilogy

MENDOCINO COAST:

Boonville Hotel
Cafe Beaujolais

Little River Inn
Little River Restaurant

CARMEL-MONTEREY-
  BIG SUR-HEARST CASTLE:

Creekside Gardens
Hermanos, Los
Nepenthe
Rigdon Hall
Rio Grill
Whaling Station

*San Francisco, Oakland and Marin County Restaurants
by type of cuisine:*

AMERICAN:
Eddie Rickenbacker's
Garden Court
Horizons
Marina's Bar and Grill

BREAKFAST:
Buena Vista Cafe
Sears'

BUFFET:
Crown Room

CALIFORNIA CUISINE:
Avenue, L'
Casa Madrona
Hayes Street Grill
Postrio

CAMBODIAN:
Angkor Wat

CHINESE (lunch only):
Tung Fong

CHINESE:
China Moon
Hong Kong Flower Lounge
Mandarin
Mike's Chinese Cuisine
Mon Kiang
Yuet Lee

FRENCH:
Castel, Le
Fleur de Lys
Jack's
Janot's
Zola's

ITALIAN:
Acquerello
Angelino
Caffe Sport

INDEX